Working the

S - A N O N

Program

SECOND EDITION

S-ANON
International

Family Groups

Working the S-Anon Program
© S-Anon International Family Groups, Inc., 2003, 2009

P.O. Box 111242
Nashville, TN 37222-1242

Library of Congress Control Number: 2002096635
ISBN # 978-0-9676637-1-5

SAN: 255-0261

S-ANON
International
Family Groups

S-Anon Conference Approved Literature
Printed in the United States of America.
For information write or call the S-Anon World Service Office:
S-Anon International Family Groups, Inc.
P.O. Box 111242
Nashville, TN 37222-1242

Phone: 615-833-3152 and 800-210-8141
E-mail: sanon@sanon.org
Web site: http://www.sanon.org

&

God, grant me the serenity

To accept the things I cannot change,

Courage to change the things I can,

And wisdom to know the difference.

&

ACKNOWLEDGMENTS

The materials excerpted from *Alcoholics Anonymous* are reprinted with permission of Alcoholics Anonymous World Services, Inc. (A.A.W.S.) Permission to reprint these excerpts does not mean that A.A.W.S. has reviewed or approved the contents of this publication, or that A.A. necessarily agrees with the views expressed herein. A.A. is a program of recovery from alcoholism only — use of these excerpts in connection with programs and activities which are patterned after A.A., but which address other problems, or in any other non-A.A. context, does not imply otherwise.

Grateful acknowledgment is made for permission to reprint the following:

Excerpts from *Alcoholics Anonymous*. Copyright 1939, 1955, 1976, 2001 by Alcoholics Anonymous World Services, Inc.: New York, NY. Reprinted by permission of Alcoholics Anonymous World Services, Inc.

Excerpts from Al-Anon Conference Approved Literature are reprinted with permission of Al-Anon Family Group Headquarters, Inc. Permission to reprint these excerpts does not mean that Al-Anon Family Group Headquarters, Inc. has reviewed or approved the contents of this publication, or that Al-Anon Family Group Headquarters, Inc. necessarily agrees with the views expressed herein. Al-Anon is a program of recovery for families and friends of alcoholics—use of these excerpts in any non Al-Anon context does not imply endorsement or affiliation by Al-Anon.

Grateful acknowledgement is made for permission to reprint the following:

Excerpt from *How Al-Anon Works for Families & Friends of Alcoholics*. Copyright 1995 by Al-Anon Family Group Headquarters, Inc.: Virginia Beach, VA. Reprinted by permission of Al-Anon Family Group Headquarters, Inc.

Excerpt from *Paths to Recovery: Al-Anon's Steps, Traditions, and Concepts*. Copyright 1997 by Al-Anon Family Group Headquarters, Inc.: Virginia Beach, VA. Reprinted by permission of Al-Anon Family Group Headquarters, Inc.

CONTENTS

❧

S-ANON CHECKLIST QUESTIONS
Are you affected by someone's sexual behavior?

৵

1. Have you felt hurt or embarrassed by someone's sexual conduct?

2. Have you secretly searched for clues about someone's sexual behavior?

3. Have you lied about or covered up another person's sexual conduct?

4. Have you had money problems because of someone's sexual behavior?

5. Have you felt betrayed or abandoned by someone you loved and trusted?

6. Are you afraid to upset the sexaholic for fear that he or she will leave you?

7. Have you tried to control somebody's sexual thoughts or behavior by doing things like throwing away pornography, dressing suggestively, or being sexual with them in order to keep them from being sexual with others?

8. Have you used sex to try to keep peace in a relationship?

9. Have you tried to convince yourself that someone else's sexual thoughts and behavior shouldn't bother you?

10. Have you felt that sex plays an all-consuming role in your relationship?

11. Have you doubted your attractiveness, your emotions, and your sanity?

12. Have you felt responsible for the sexual behavior of another person?

13. Have you felt angry and/or stupid for not knowing about someone's sexual acting out behavior?

14. Have you engaged in uncomfortable, unwanted, or physically dangerous sexual behavior?

15. Have you ever thought about or attempted suicide because of someone's sexual behavior?

16. Has your preoccupation with someone's sexual thoughts and behavior affected your relationships with your children, your co-workers, and/or other friends or family members?

17. Have you neglected your physical and/or emotional health while in a relationship?

18. Have you helped someone get out of jail or other legal trouble, or feared legal action as a result of his or her sexual behavior?

19. Have you blamed other people, such as friends or sexual partners, society in general, his/her job, religion, or birth family for someone's sexual behavior?

20. Have you felt confused about what is true when talking with someone about his or her sexual thoughts or behavior?

21. Have you avoided painful emotions by using drugs, alcohol, or food or by being too busy?

22. Have you ever felt that someone was inappropriately attracted to you or your children?

23. Have you felt alone or too ashamed to ask for help?

If you can answer "yes" to some of these checklist questions, you may find help in S-Anon.

THE TWELVE STEPS OF S-ANON

Working the Twelve Steps of S-Anon, that is putting the principles of the Steps into practice in our lives, brings about our recovery from the effects of living with the sexaholism of a family member or friend.

1. We admitted we were powerless over sexaholism—that our lives had become unmanageable.

2. Came to believe that a Power greater than ourselves could restore us to sanity.

3. Made a decision to turn our will and our lives over to the care of God *as we understood Him.*

4. Made a searching and fearless moral inventory of ourselves.

5. Admitted to God, to ourselves, and to another human being the exact nature of our wrongs.

6. Were entirely ready to have God remove all these defects of character.

7. Humbly asked Him to remove our shortcomings.

8. Made a list of all persons we had harmed, and became willing to make amends to them all.

9. Made direct amends to such people wherever possible, except when to do so would injure them or others.

10. Continued to take personal inventory and when we were wrong promptly admitted it.

11. Sought through prayer and meditation to improve our conscious contact with God *as we understood Him,* praying only for knowledge of His will for us and the power to carry that out.

12. Having had a spiritual awakening as the result of these Steps, we tried to carry this message to others, and to practice these principles in all our affairs.

THE TWELVE STEPS OF ALCOHOLICS ANONYMOUS:

1. We admitted we were powerless over alcohol—that our lives had become unmanageable. 2. Came to believe that a Power greater than ourselves could restore us to sanity. 3. Made a decision to turn our will and our lives over to the care of God *as we understood Him*. 4. Made a searching and fearless moral inventory of ourselves. 5. Admitted to God, to ourselves, and to another human being the exact nature of our wrongs. 6. Were entirely ready to have God remove all these defects of character. 7. Humbly asked Him to remove our shortcomings. 8. Made a list of all persons we had harmed, and became willing to make amends to them all. 9. Made direct amends to such people wherever possible, except when to do so would injure them or others. 10. Continued to take personal inventory and when we were wrong promptly admitted it. 11. Sought through prayer and meditation to improve our conscious contact with God *as we understood Him*, praying only for knowledge of His will for us and the power to carry that out. 12. Having had a spiritual awakening as the result of these Steps, we tried to carry this message to alcoholics, and to practice these principles in all our affairs.

THE TWELVE TRADITIONS OF S-ANON

❧

The Traditions guide the growth and health of our groups and our world wide fellowship. Our group experience suggests that the unity of the S-Anon Family Groups depends upon our adherence to the following Traditions.

1. Our common welfare should come first; personal progress for the greatest number depends upon unity.

2. For our group purpose there is but one authority—a loving God as He may express Himself in our group conscience. Our leaders are but trusted servants—they do not govern.

3. The relatives of sexaholics, when gathered together for mutual aid, may call themselves an S-Anon Family Group, provided that, as a group, they have no other affiliation. The only requirement for membership is that there be a problem of sexaholism in a relative or friend.

4. Each group should be autonomous, except in matters affecting another group or S-Anon or SA as a whole.

5. Each S-Anon Family Group has but one purpose: to help families of sexaholics. We do this by practicing the Twelve Steps of S-Anon, by encouraging and understanding our sexaholic relatives, and by welcoming and giving comfort to the families of sexaholics.

6. Our S-Anon Family Groups ought never endorse, finance, or lend our name to any outside enterprise, lest problems of money, property, and prestige divert us from our primary spiritual aim. Although a separate entity, we should always cooperate with Sexaholics Anonymous.

7. Every group ought to be fully self-supporting, declining outside contributions.

8. S-Anon Twelfth Step work should remain forever non-professional, but our service centers may employ special workers.

9. Our groups, as such, ought never be organized; but we may create service boards or committees directly responsible to those they serve.

10. The S-Anon Family Groups have no opinion on outside issues; hence our name ought never be drawn into public controversy.

11. Our public relations policy is based on attraction rather than promotion; we need always maintain personal anonymity at the level of press, radio, TV and films. We need guard with special care the anonymity of all S-Anon and SA members.

12. Anonymity is the spiritual foundation of all our Traditions, ever reminding us to place principles above personalities.

THE TWELVE CONCEPTS OF S-ANON

๛

S-Anon's Twelve Concepts of Service illustrate that Twelfth Step work can be accomplished on a broad scale. The Concepts are guidelines for the World Service Office staff, the Board of Trustees, standing committees, and World Service Conference members to relate to each other and to groups.

1. The ultimate responsibility and authority for S-Anon world services belongs to the S-Anon groups.

2. The S-Anon Family Groups have delegated complete administrative and operational authority to their Conference and its service arms.

3. The Right of Decision makes effective leadership possible.

4. Participation is the key to harmony

5. The Rights of Appeal and Petition protect minorities and assure that they be heard.

6. The Conference acknowledges the primary administrative responsibility of the Trustees.

7. The Trustees have legal rights while the rights of the Conference are Traditional.

8. The Board of Trustees delegates full authority for routine management of the S-Anon headquarters to its executive committees.

9. Good personal leadership at all service levels is a necessity. In the field of World Service, the Board of Trustees assumes the primary leadership.

10. Service responsibility is balanced by carefully defined service authority and double-headed management is avoided.

11. The World Service Office is composed of an Executive Director and staff members.

12. The spiritual foundation for S-Anon's World Services is contained in the General Warranties of the Conference, Article 12 of the Charter.

The General Warranties of the Conference

In all proceedings the World Service Conference of S-Anon shall observe the spirit of the Traditions:

1. That only sufficient operating funds, including an ample reserve, be its prudent financial principle;

2. That no Conference member shall be placed in unqualified authority over other members;

3. That all decisions be reached by discussion, vote, and whenever possible, by unanimity;

4. That no Conference action ever be personally punitive or an incitement to public controversy;

5. That though the Conference serves S-Anon, it shall never perform any act of government; and like the fellowship of S-Anon which it serves, it shall always remain democratic in thought and action.

INTRODUCTION

S-Anon is a program of recovery from the effects of sexaholism, based on the Twelve Steps and the Twelve Traditions of S-Anon, for the families and friends of sexaholics. The Steps and Traditions are based upon the Twelve Steps and Traditions of Alcoholics Anonymous, the original Twelve-Step Program. The "primary purpose" of S-Anon, found in our Fifth Tradition, is to help families and friends of sexaholics. We do this by "practicing the Twelve Steps of S-Anon, by encouraging and understanding our sexaholic relatives, and by welcoming and giving comfort to the families of sexaholics."

We have found that there is little likelihood of recovery in our relationships with others, nor were we able to help anyone including ourselves, until we first examined some of our own attitudes and past actions in the light of the Twelve Steps of S-Anon. We found that there was no "quick fix" or easy way out. We often use the term "working" the program to signify our acceptance of this reality. We did, however, find a measure of relief as soon as we shared our burden with other S-Anon members who understood our pain. We found that we were better able to help ourselves and others, when we committed ourselves to the principles that lead to spiritual and emotional growth we heard described in S-Anon meetings and in S-Anon Conference Approved Literature. We couldn't have imagined when we first came to S-Anon that our lives would one day be filled with joy, serenity, and peace, but that has been the experience of countless S-Anon members. Without hesitation, we invite you to join us on our journey of recovery.

This book combines new material with a significant amount of information and sharing previously published in S-Anon pamphlets. We hope that it will be helpful to have all this material compiled in a single publication, *Working the S-Anon Program.*

This book is organized into four parts, each of which is related to an important area of our recovery. The first three parts contain brief explanatory material, followed by sharing contributed by S-Anon members on each topic. To promote clarity, member sharing in each section is indented. The fourth part provides material used in S-Anon meetings.

- **Part 1** describes the tools we use (actions we take, principles we integrate into our lives, and attitudes we develop) to begin and enhance our personal recovery.
- **Part 2** contains sharing from S-Anon members on their experiences of healing and recovery in their relationships with the sexaholics in their lives and with others.
- **Part 3** focuses on ways we can carry the S-Anon message of recovery to those who still suffer from the effects of sexaholism.
- **Part 4** contains the suggested S-Anon meeting format, complete with suggested readings.

We acknowledge here with humility and gratitude our debt of thanks to those who have preceded us in recovery in other Twelve Step programs. We occasionally quote from Alcoholics Anonymous and Al-Anon literature in an attempt to tap into the rich heritage of recovery described therein. Most of us find that AA and Al-Anon literature can offer hope and insight as we work the S-Anon program.

FORWARD TO THE
SECOND EDITION

As S-Anon members, we have been affected by sexaholism in various ways. It is our common problems that have brought us together. Through working the S-Anon program, we have found hope and solutions to our problems. We have learned that we need help for ourselves no matter what the sexaholic in our lives decides to do regarding his or her problem. We have admitted that we needed to focus on our own attitudes and behaviors and that we needed recovery from our own progressive illness.

In the Second Edition, we have revised some of the original text to more clearly keep the focus on our own recovery. Several new shares have been added. All of the sharing reflects the experiences of recovering S-Anon members. We are grateful for all who have contributed their stories and experiences to make this book possible. We trust that this book carries a message of hope and recovery for those who still suffer from the effects on them of another person's sexaholism. As we have learned to trust a Power greater than ourselves and work the S-Anon Program, one day at a time, we have found many gifts along the way.

Several programs are available for recovery from sexaholism and, as is suggested in the Sixth Tradition, S-Anon does not take a position on which recovery program is appropriate for any particular sexaholic. S-Anon does cooperate with Sexaholics Anonymous (SA) for certain events, but some of our members have friends and relatives who work another program or no program at all.

The Second Edition includes S-Anon's Twelve Concepts of Service, reflecting our growth as an organization since our beginnings in the early 1980's. The Board of Trustees was established in 2000, and the World Service Conference in 2003. *The S-Anon/S-Ateen Service Manual* replaced the *Group Handbook* in 2007. The S-Anon Checklist questions were revised in 2008. We now have four S-Anon books available as part of our Conference Approved Literature: *S-Anon Twelve Steps*; *Exploring the Wonders of Recovery: A Companion Guide to S-Anon Twelve Steps*; *Reflections of Hope*; and, *Working the S-Anon Program*. S-Anon has expanded to include members across the United States and other countries. It is difficult to know how many members there actually are. As of this printing there are approximately 240 registered S-Anon groups in the United States and Canada. Many members meet through electronic media as well.

We celebrate that this Second Edition represents our progress, not perfection, as we journey together exploring the wonders of serenity, dignity, and emotional growth.

PERSONAL RECOVERY

℀

Using the Tools
of the
S-Anon Program

The tools of the S-Anon Program are actions we take, principles we use, and attitudes we develop. The actions we take include going to meetings, sharing with others, having a sponsor and being a sponsor, reading S-Anon Conference Approved Literature, writing down our thoughts and feelings, and being of service. The principles we use are found in the Twelve Steps and Twelve Traditions of S-Anon. They include ideas aimed at allowing us to develop spiritually, as we are guided by the Higher Power of our understanding. The basic attitudes that we aim toward developing are honesty, open-mindedness, and willingness. These tools, when used with the Twelve Steps of S-Anon, help our lives to gradually become more serene and fulfilling. Examples of how the tools are used come directly from S-Anon members themselves.

Many of us found that before we could begin to use the tools of S-Anon, we had to let go of, or at least loosen our grip on the "old tools" that may have helped us survive, but simply did not work well anymore. The old tools may have included denial, obsession with the sexaholic, covering up the problem, isolation, rage, and manipulation. In letting go of the old tools, we were able to try new, more effective ways to aid us in recovery. While letting go was at times frightening, we saw that it was the only way to achieve the serenity we longed to have. "We let go of the problem, the need to know what will happen and when, the obsession with other people's choices, the thoughts and concerns that waste our time and energy because we cannot resolve them by ourselves. And we let God take care of them."[1]

Each member uses the tools that work best for him or her. We have found that some things that did not work for us in early recovery became mainstays later on. We use what helps us today and leave the rest for later. We urge you to give serious consideration to how you can use some of these tools to help your recovery from the effects of sexaholism since these tools have been indispensable to our recovery. We believe that the quote below from the Big Book of Alcoholics Anonymous says it best:

> There is a solution. Almost none of us liked the self-searching, the leveling of our pride, the confession of shortcomings which the process requires for its successful consummation. But we saw that it really worked in others, and we had come to believe in the hopelessness and futility of life as we had been living it. When, therefore, we were approached by those in whom the problem had been solved, there was nothing left for us but to pick up the simple kit of spiritual tools laid at our feet.[2]

---

[1] *How Al-Anon Works for Families & Friends of Alcoholics*, p. 76

[2] *Alcoholics Anonymous*, p. 25

TAKING ACTION

GOING TO MEETINGS

Meetings are a vital part of the S-Anon Program, providing us with the opportunity to identify and confirm common problems and to hear the experience, strength, and hope of others. Meetings give us a place where we can be ourselves and be unconditionally accepted. For those of us who have access to them, regular attendance at meetings is an important tool in working the program and staying "sober" in S-Anon. To find an S-Anon meeting in your area you may check our website, www.sanon.org, or you may call the S-Anon World Service Office (WSO). It took courage to go to meetings, but we found it well worth the effort. We found that when we took positive action, help was there for us in S-Anon.

When possible we attend meetings at S-Anon Conventions and other gatherings that are held throughout the United States and other countries. S-Anon International Conventions are held in the United States and Canada.* These events have become an important support for many S-Anon members. They also serve as a gathering place for the largest number of S-Anon members from a broad base of experience. Some of us have found the Conventions to be a good place to find a sponsor and to broaden our S-Anon support. Attendees have the opportunity to go to many meetings, on various topics, as well as meet S-Anon members from other states and countries.

Some of us have begun to work the S-Anon Program without any S-Anon meetings in our area. We may have found attending "meetings" through the electronic media helpful. Contact the WSO for information.

---

* S-Anon Conventions and other gatherings are frequently held in cooperation with the Sexaholics Anonymous (SA) Fellowship.

Attending other Twelve Step programs that offer open meetings may also be helpful in breaking our isolation and strengthening our spirits. The word "open" means that anyone interested in that particular fellowship, may sit in on the meeting being held. "Closed" meetings are for those who qualify as members for a particular fellowship. These other Twelve Step meetings; however, cannot take the place of face-to-face meetings with other S-Anon members. Please respect other fellowships' open and closed meeting guidelines.

After we have gained support and experience, some of us have started meetings in our local areas. Additional information about meetings may be found in the *S-Anon/S-Ateen Service Manual* in the section "How S-Anon and S-Ateen Groups Work," and the companion guide entitled, "How to Start a Meeting." The meeting format and readings are available in the *S-Anon/S-Ateen Service Manual* and in Part Four of this book.

•   •   •

MEMBERS SHARE

Finding Help... When I heard "keep coming back" at the end of meetings, I felt the tug to come back even though I felt discouraged with my situation. I came back (trudged back) and found help and friendship. Now I am aware that I need these meetings and need to continue to hear the other group members' experience.

Not Alone... I don't know what I would have done during the months after my husband told me he was a sexaholic if I had not had the support of my meetings. Because there was only one S-Anon meeting in my area, I also attended some "open" Al-Anon meetings for added support. The meetings assured me that my feelings were real and that I wasn't alone.

Came to Believe... I heard at a meeting that "at first we came; then we came to; then we came to believe." Going to meetings was the beginning of my recovery—and the beginning of trusting that a Power greater than myself could help me.

Humility... My first S-Anon meeting was at an International Convention since there were no S-Anon meetings in my area. My husband, who was in recovery for his sexaholism, wanted to go to the convention and wanted me to go, too. I was scared. I thought I wouldn't want to look anyone in the eye. I feared there would be sex addicts hanging around looking for trouble. Going to the convention, however, was a life-changing experience for me. I heard honesty and courage from both sexaholics and their family members and friends. I had a spiritual renewal as I humbled myself and realized I was really no better or worse than anyone else there.

Practicing Skills... Meetings have been a safe learning environment for me. For example, to ask someone not to share from non-Conference Approved Literature in a meeting was tough for a people-pleaser like me. Yet, developing the courage to do that helped me work through this and other issues that were problematic for me. I'm grateful to be able to practice these new skills in the safety of the group.

Recovery Boost... S-Anon International Conventions have become a wonderful life-line for me. When I actively participate at a Convention, I get a boost in my own recovery by being with other S-Anon members. Conventions are where I hear other stories like my personal story. I am reminded that I am not alone. By going to open Sexaholics Anonymous speaker meetings at the Convention, I am able to hear the stories of recovering sexaholics and how the disease of sexaholism manifested and impacted their lives. These gatherings have been a very healing experience and have helped me grow spiritually in all my relationships: Higher Power, spouse, family, and friends. The International S-Anon Conventions have become so important to me that I plan my vacations around them.

Real Growth... At one of the open speaker meetings, I first truly heard the perspective of the addict in my life. From the lips of a stranger, I began to understand the addict as a fellow spirit suffering from the effects of sexaholism. I felt real growth in my ability to "encourage and understand my sexaholic relatives," as suggested in our Fifth Tradition. I believe I am now much better able to "welcome and give comfort to the families of sexaholics."

SHARING WITH OTHERS

While no one is ever obliged to share, we have found that sharing is an important part of working the program. We relate our experience—the painful and pleasant; our strength—that which keeps us going; and our hope—the positive viewpoint we see even if it is simply surrendering to our Higher Power. Remaining silent is always our option, but eventually we found that sharing with other members and with a sponsor helped us to grow. (See the next section for more information on Sponsorship.)

Sharing Through Meetings
Sharing during a meeting or with someone after a meeting are good ways to share in S-Anon. By sharing, we take part in the fellowship, coming out of the isolation that is common among us. We take responsibility for ourselves when we make an effort to share as much as we can with another member about what we are experiencing. We ask for telephone numbers from members of S-Anon so we can share during the week.

Sharing by Telephone
Between meetings we make telephone calls to members of S-Anon when we need to reach out for help or just need to hear someone's "recovery" point-of-view. Many of us hesitated to call another member on the telephone because we felt we were a burden, but reaching out benefits both the caller and the person who receives the call. If someone is unable to talk at the time we call, we can arrange another time to talk or make another call. We learn how to set limits in S-Anon, and we learn to respect the limits of others. This is growth for us.

Sharing by E-mail
Meeting with other S-Anon members via E-mail is a valuable and important tool especially for those who live far from a meeting. Making contact with S-Anon members who understand and can share their similar experiences is liberating and gives hope. If you

are interested in the S-Anon E-mail group, please contact the S-Anon World Service Office. We have found, however, that it is worth any amount of effort to attend a face-to-face meeting, even if it is inconvenient or a distance from our home.

• • •

MEMBERS SHARE

Starting Small... I listened to people sharing at S-Anon meetings and felt like they were telling my story. I could relate so well to the feelings they expressed. Yet it was a hurdle for me to get over feeling totally inadequate about sharing. I often choked up with emotion, making sharing impossible. So I started very small—talking to people after the meeting, especially people with stories to which I could relate. Eventually I could share at meetings. Now, when someone comes to me after a meeting and thanks me for my sharing, I am amazed and thank my Higher Power.

Reaching Out... Sometimes I make calls to talk about decisions (not an easy task for me). I don't want advice; I just need a listening ear. Sharing with someone who understands and can suggest some direction in working the Steps is so helpful.

Vacationing... Once, while on vacation, I felt some panic and decided to make a program call. Two calls and two answering machines later, I felt better knowing I was taking care of myself by reaching out, even though I wasn't able to reach anyone in person.

Sharing on the Steps... Five other S-Anon members and I formed our own Step study group. We met for an hour before one of our weekly meetings. We shared thoughts and insights from our written Step work and helped each other stay on track.

Feeling Good... It's O.K. to call with good news, too. I sometimes get scared when things are going well for me. I need reassurance that as I continue to progress in my recovery, I will have many more good days than bad days. It doesn't mean that I'm in denial about something if I'm feeling good.

Fellowship... Our group has had a tradition of going out for coffee after the meeting. This fellowship time is not required, but it's certainly helped me break out of isolation and take time for myself. It also gives newcomers an opportunity for fellowship and a relaxed setting in which to ask questions about how the program works.

E-Mail... It seems ironic that the thing that contributed so much trouble in my marriage and was my partner's tool for acting out, is the very thing that helps me so much. The Internet has been great for me to communicate with other S-Anon members. There are no meetings in my area yet, and until a meeting gets started, the Internet meeting is giving me the feeling that I am not alone on this difficult journey.

Overcoming Fear... I have come to believe that the best way that I can carry the message is sharing with other people in a meeting. I was more familiar with going into a group and blending into the woodwork. I was afraid of saying the wrong thing, hurting somebody's feelings, or making a fool of myself. My thoughts were always focused on how other people were seeing me, so sometimes the best approach for me was just to not speak. At my first meeting I thought, "I don't know how I'll ever be able to do this." But someone told me, "If you want to get better, you have to raise your hand. You have to share what's going on with you." And I did, and I do. And it really does work.

FINDING AND BEING A SPONSOR

A sking someone to sponsor us may seem like an overwhelming step, but we found it a vital one in working the program. The S-Anon leaflet "Sponsorship in S-Anon" states, "In S-Anon, a sponsor is simply a person in the program who can help us work the Steps by sharing how they have worked, or are working these Steps in their own lives. No one is required to have a sponsor. It is a suggestion based upon the experiences of members who find that when they become very confused or frustrated, it is most helpful to have one person in S-Anon who knows them well." This does not mean the sponsor is an authority figure or someone who tells the sponsee what to do. A sponsor is someone who will guide and support the sponsee as the sponsee makes his/her own decisions. A sponsor is also someone to talk with about the personal, lengthy details of our story that may not be appropriate to share at a meeting. An S-Anon sponsor encourages sponsees to work the whole S-Anon Program.

The person we ask to be our sponsor is usually someone with more experience in the program than we have—someone who continues to do Step work, attends meetings regularly, and works the S-Anon program with their own sponsor. Most of us find it works best to choose a sponsor of our same gender. The most important thing is that the relationship between the sponsor and sponsee is based on honesty and trust. Sponsorship is not just a tool for newcomers to consider. It does not matter how long a person has been a member of S-Anon; it is never too late to ask someone to be our sponsor. Through sponsorship, we give to others what has been so generously given to us.

S-Anon does not train, screen, or endorse individuals as sponsors, but we do have some members who are available long-distance to sponsor others through the Twelve Steps. This form of sponsorship would probably mean regular long-distance telephone calls that are usually paid for by the sponsee. Members who have used this form of sponsorship report that often the telephone conversations begin with a prayer, Step work, and review of Conference Approved Literature, keeping any discussion of current issues for later in the call, if possible. This puts the focus on resolving the S-Anon problem, and makes it less likely that we will be distracted by its many symptoms. If you are interested in either being a long-distance sponsor or getting a long-distance sponsor, please contact the S-Anon World Service Office.

• • •

MEMBERS SHARE

Understanding... I asked a member to be my sponsor because I felt I needed to connect with someone regularly. I don't talk to her every day, but she has heard my story more completely than anyone else, and when I call her in a particularly hard time, she understands.

Better Late than Never... It took me nearly five years in S-Anon to get a sponsor. I'm not sure if it was pride saying I didn't really need one, or if it was insecurity telling me nobody would want to or have the time to be my sponsor. I finally asked someone after an S-Anon International Convention, and I was relieved when she agreed. She lives in another state so I write and call her. Getting a sponsor wasn't so painful after all. I don't know why I waited so long.

Helping Ourselves by Helping Others... Dr. Bob, one of the founders of AA, used to say that sponsoring others helps us whether the sponsee gets better or not. If they fail to work the program, they show us what happens if we relapse into our past means of coping. If they stay and work the program they show us that the program works. Either way, they help us.

Practicing... Being a sponsor has been an important tool for growth in the program. When working with sponsees, I have to actively practice the principles that develop the skills I need to live serenely: working the Steps and Traditions, setting boundaries, having compassion, and relying on God.

Connecting… Each of the S-Anon groups in our area has a newcomers' table for people who are coming to their first meetings. Newcomers hear First Step stories and get connected with temporary sponsors who commit to calling them. It helps newcomers feel that they are a part of the group and it helps other S-Anon members grow in their recovery. As we listen to newcomers, we can remember what our lives used to be like—and can be like again without recovery. We realize that we do have valuable experience, strength, and hope to share.

You can find more suggestions and experience on sponsorship in Part Three of this book.

USING THE SLOGANS

Slogans help many of us focus our thoughts on positive attitudes, especially during difficult and stressful times. Although at first they may seem trite or too simplistic; they are a form of shorthand, easily remembered in times of need, that bring to mind important principles of recovery. They also remind us that our attitude is an important key to recovery. Here are some of the slogans S-Anon members use:

Let Go and Let God
Easy Does It
Live and Let Live
First Things First
One Day at a Time
Keep It Simple
Think
Progress, Not Perfection
Listen and Learn
There, but for the Grace of God, Go I
How Important Is It?
If You Spot It, You've Got It
Act As If...
It Works When You Work It
Keep Coming Back
H.A.L.T.
This Too Shall Pass

•   •   •

MEMBERS SHARE

Let Go and Let God... I wish I could just surrender my fears once and for all. I think I have let go of a concern or fear and a few moments later I realize I'm trying to figure it out again. So I breathe the slogan again—Let Go and Let God. Some days I think I pray it hundreds of times. It helps me find peace. I also keep in mind, that letting go by placing the situation in God's care, is not the same as giving up. Letting go is not buckling under pressure; it is placing my concerns in God's care and surrendering to God's will.

First Things First... A slogan I'm using a lot lately is First Things First. I tend to get overwhelmed by the number of tasks in front of me. Using this slogan helps me not only prioritize the things I need to do, but also to keep some balance in my life. I am reminded that "First Things" might include taking the time to eat properly, participating in something I enjoy, or taking time to relax, praying and meditating, or working a Step.

Act As If... I have a difficult time being gentle, particularly with my spouse. The slogan Act As If... helps me to act more gently, even though my heart may not really be in a loving place. The amazing thing is that after I've taken a gentle action, I actually feel more gentle and loving.

It Works When You Work It... Sometimes when I'm feeling confused and hopeless, I wonder if the Twelve Steps are helping me at all. I find myself distrusting the program. It's then that I remind myself that It Works When You Work It . I reflect on all the members in the fellowship and make an effort to speak to them and hear their stories of the countless miracles of recovery. Then I'm reassured that I'm following the right path, and I am motivated to move forward in working the program.

H.A.L.T. ... Recognizing when I am Hungry, Angry, Lonely, or Tired has been valuable to me as a quick assessment. When I feel old thinking and frustration creeping in, I am most grateful that this slogan directs me to self-care and responsiveness rather than reactivity.

This Too Shall Pass... As an S-Anon who used to despair when confronted with change, this slogan provides me with the valuable reminder that change is a part of living a real life, and nothing is forever. No happiness or unhappiness lasts forever. No situation, however painful or glorious, lasts forever. No relationship lasts forever in a particular form; all real relationships, whether group or individual, have their seasons and phases. I used to fear that my pain would never end, or hope that things would always be a certain way. Now, when I find myself thinking in terms of "always" and "never," it is a signal to me that I have forgotten that change is normal and that "this too shall pass."

Easy Does It... This slogan helps me the most when I find myself trying to force solutions. It is so hard for me to stand back, mind my own business, and let situations work themselves out in God's time (and often without my help!). The slogan also helps me when I become convinced that I should be further along in recovery than I am, or that I am not doing enough work on my recovery or enough service to my group. Easy Does It reminds me to be good to myself and let a Higher Power lead me.

One Day at a Time... For a person who used to spend huge blocks of time regretting the past and worrying about the future, this slogan helps me every day to bring my focus back to this one day, today, and concentrate on what I can do today to make my life more serene and fulfilling. For me, the key to solving today's problems lies more in doing one small thing today – saying a prayer, calling my sponsor, reading some Conference Approved Literature – than in making plans for what I might do to solve them tomorrow, or dwelling upon what I could have done in the past to prevent them.

Progress Not Perfection... This slogan comes from the Big Book of Alcoholics Anonymous, and it appears right after the listing of the Twelve Steps: "No one among us has been able to maintain anything like perfect adherence to these principles. We are not saints. The point is, that we are willing to grow along spiritual lines. The principles we have set down are guides to progress. We claim spiritual progress rather than spiritual perfection." [3] Thus, this slo-

---

[3] *Alcoholics Anonymous*, p. 60

gan reminds me that in S-Anon I am not asked to achieve perfection; I am just asked to make progress in becoming the person my Higher Power made me to be.

READING S-ANON LITERATURE

S-Anon Conference Approved Literature represents the S-Anon point of view regarding our common problems that arise from the effects on us of another person's sexaholism. Most of us have found it helpful to read the experiences of others who have found hope and recovery through applying the S-Anon Twelve Steps and the S-Anon principles to their lives. Our literature is written by S-Anon members for S-Anon members and offers the best experience about recovery from the family disease of sexaholism. Each piece of literature is written and edited by a volunteer committee of S-Anon Members. Another group of volunteers reads the literature and offers suggestions and feedback as it is being developed. Literature becomes approved—or Conference Approved—through a deliberate process of reviewing, revising, and approving by representative members of S-Anon. S-Anon is patterned after Al-Anon and Alcoholics Anonymous (AA), and we find that studying literature from these other fellowships can be helpful as well. At the time of this printing S-Anon, Sexaholics Anonymous, Al-Anon, and AA literature are Conference Approved for use in our meetings. To receive an updated S-Anon Literature Order Form, check with the S-Anon World Service Office or visit our web site (www.sanon.org). Some other language translations of literature may also be available.

• • •

MEMBERS SHARE

Serenity Boost... I always have Conference Approved Literature with me. I have various pamphlets that I can keep in my purse. I pull one out if I have a few spare minutes, such as waiting for an appointment. This gives me a little "boost of serenity" and helps me onto a more positive track. It sometimes enables me to see opportunity in a situation. I am finding that I always get what I need when I am willing to reach for a tool to work my program.

Focus on the Solution... Our Conference Approved Literature has been such a help to me. Like so many others, when I came to S-Anon in crisis, I tried to read everything in print on this addiction. But, it was in our S-Anon literature that I found similar experiences that really hit home with me. It consistently focused on the solution rather than the problem, and the solution was what I really needed, not further analysis of the problem.

Listening with New Ears... When I first came to S-Anon, I was frustrated that we would frequently study parts of S-Anon literature over and over. But as I really started to work the program, my frustration eased. I found that the literature continued to speak to me as I grew in recovery. Many times I thought, "Wait! That must be a new part to that reading!" No, it wasn't, I just heard it with "new ears!"

Less Alone... I get a lot out of regularly reading program literature like S-Anon's daily reader, *Reflections of Hope*, or Al-Anon's *Courage to Change*. I read until something strikes me as being "right-on" for where I am today. Then I think about what that means to me. When I don't have the courage to reach out to another S-Anon member, sometimes reaching for a book helps me feel less alone and vulnerable.

A Lifeline... Literature has been a lifeline for me. I have no one closer than three hours away and no meeting to attend regularly. I use the literature and phone calls as a way to keep the program alive. The literature reminds me that I'm not alone and that there are others like me who have faced and overcome the same struggles, depression, and pain, and who can offer me their experience, strength, and hope.

The Essence of My Experience... I have read many different pieces of S-Anon Conference Approved Literature in addition to the opening readings for S-Anon meetings, and I have found them to be a tremendous help to me because they are rooted in recovery. Many great books on relationships and self-help are commercially available, but they do not get to the essence of my struggle—learning how to make healthier choices by letting God be in control of me.

The Gift of Recovery... Today, I feel free to experience more and more of life as I live it one day at a time, increasingly free from the effects of sexaholism. I am becoming more accepting of myself and find I have stopped comparing myself to other women. The program has given me all of this through the literature only, as I have never spoken with another member or gone to a meeting due to my remote location.

WRITING AND USING A JOURNAL

There are many ways to use the tool of writing; our writing is as individual as each of us. One thing is clear; writing is a great way to get in touch with our feelings. Writing things down helps us understand our actions and reactions at a depth that thinking and talking may not reveal. Keeping a journal, writing letters (sent or unsent), writing out our Step work, and composing prayers and meditations are helpful ways to use this tool. When we want to work on a Step, we have found it helpful to write down our feelings, difficulties, and progress on that Step. With Step One, for example, many of us wrote down the ways in which our lives had become unmanageable and how we had reacted to another's sexaholism. What events led up to our admission that we were powerless over sexaholism? How did we act when we still thought that we could control sexaholism or that we were the cause of the disease? We have also written on questions that are in our S-Anon literature, like the *S-Anon Twelve Steps*. We may want to use *Exploring the Wonders of Recovery: A Companion Guide to S-Anon Twelve Steps,* as it is in a workbook format with space for writing on each question from *S-Anon Twelve Steps.* The S-Anon Checklist Questions found in the pamphlet "Is S-Anon for You?" and on page vii in this book may also serve as a guide for writing. Writing on questions like these has helped us to grow.

•   •   •

MEMBERS SHARE

Getting Clarity... I have found writing particularly useful when I'm experiencing strong feelings. Letting the angry, sad, or anxious words flow onto the paper seems to get them out of my head, allowing me to experience clarity. I often find great insight when I leave the writing for several hours (or days), then reread it. The real issue is often apparent after the emotions I was experiencing at the moment have quieted.

Freedom to Share... I have felt unable to share verbally some of my most shameful experiences. Yet not "voicing" these experiences kept me isolated with my pain. Writing in detail about those things released me from a lot of the shame. After a short time had passed, I was able to share the experiences with my sponsor. Writing gave me a feeling of freedom I had not experienced, and continues to help me release my pain.

Writing Step Work... I am glad my sponsor suggested writing down my work with the Steps. Spending the time writing my thoughts down has provided a much deeper understanding than just thinking through the Steps.

Letting Go... I find it helpful to write down my worries, cares, and impossible situations on slips of paper and physically place them in a God Bag (I've also heard of God Boxes and God Jars). It helps me to symbolically put into God's care the things I don't need to carry around.

10th Step Writing... Some members write a 10th Step inventory at the end of each day, answering questions like the following: Was I resentful, selfish, dishonest, or afraid? Do I owe someone an apology? Have I kept something to myself which should have been discussed with another person at once? Was I kind and loving toward all? What could I have done better? Was I thinking of myself most of the time, or was I thinking of what I could do for others? List three things I did well today; three things I am grateful for; three things I did for others. Describe one spiritual victory or spiritual high point experienced today.

BEING OF SERVICE

How is service to others going to help me? As with many spiritual tools, service works subtly. In some unexplained way, taking action to serve others not only helps the group and S-Anon as a whole, but it also helps us to feel part of the group. Service helps us to be responsible for our own recovery, to connect, and to begin making progress in recovery. We found it was important to establish a balanced level of service we were comfortable with and avoid substituting busy "helping" for focusing on ourselves and our recovery. It is okay to check with another S-Anon member or with our sponsor if we need to clarify our motives.

When we felt ready, we found that doing service work was a way we were able to help carry the S-Anon message to others, as described in our Twelfth Step: "Having had a spiritual awakening as the result of these Steps, we tried to carry this message to others, and to practice these principles in all our affairs." Service work can include many different activities, some of which can be done long before we actually "get to" Step Twelve. For example, we can set up chairs for a meeting, work with a convention committee, be a contact person, lead a meeting, or act as group treasurer or literature person, to name a few. (For more on service, see Part Three, "Carrying the S-Anon Message.")

•   •   •

MEMBERS SHARE

Easy Does It... When I first came to Twelve-Step meetings, I felt so exhausted that I couldn't volunteer for anything. I couldn't even read without crying or losing my breath. My S-Anon group never pushed me to do something I didn't want to do, and for that I was very grateful. I don't really know how it came about, but one day I felt comfortable taking the key to open up the building for the meeting. Eventually, after many months and miraculous growth I even led a meeting.

Growth through Service... Service has contributed to my growth in some important ways. It has helped me develop skills that I have taken outside my meeting into other parts of my life. I make it a habit now to volunteer regularly for different service opportunities. (Our meeting uses a calendar where members can sign up in advance for service work.) I do my best to practice what we say at our meeting closing—we share what we have, "so we may keep what we've been given."

We Are All Responsible... I'm grateful to the member who helped me understand that we are all responsible for the meetings. I had been coming to the group about six months when she said to me, "I think it's your turn to lead the meeting." I said, "But I don't know how." She said, "That's O.K. I didn't either, but I'll help you." I finally saw that to keep what I was getting, I had to do my part and give it away, too.

Being There... Without the service work of many members, we would not have meetings or the S-Anon Fellowship. No one would have been there when I needed help. I came to understand that if I wanted recovery, I needed to do more than take what was given freely at meetings. I needed to contribute my part to carrying out our primary purpose: to help families and friends of sexaholics.

Sharing the Opportunities... I have found that service work means not only helping with activities and their organization, but also involving others in the service work. I began by inviting newer members to help me lead a newcomer breakout group. Later I had to resign as my group's treasurer and literature person because I was going back to school and my classes were on meeting night. Others were hesitant to take on this service work because they "didn't know how." So I wrote down basic guidelines and offered these as well as my time to answer questions. Then, I placed the treasury and literature order supplies on the table at my second to last meeting with this group. Sometimes others need a gentle nudge to realize how they can be of service.

Gifts of Service... Over the years I have been a member of S-Anon, I have come to enjoy many things about the program, but one of the most enjoyable things—and one I have learned the most from—has been my service on the fellowship's volunteer Literature Committee. I have learned so much about the principles and the Traditions of the program by working with others on the committee—working through differences of opinion as we craft literature. I also have gained some wonderful friendships that I treasure—all through being of service.

How Much Responsibility?... Coming into S-Anon, I was used to having a lot of responsibility. I had developed this role for me as the sexaholic became more and more irresponsible, and I felt resentful most of the time. Initially, I needed to see a group of people function without my help. My S-Anon group did very well. Eventually, I could choose to help or not to help, without falling into resentment or feeling overly responsible.

PRACTICING PROGRAM PRINCIPLES IN OUR LIVES

WORKING THE TWELVE STEPS OF S-ANON

Working the Twelve Steps of S-Anon means putting the principles of the Steps into practice in our lives. This is what brings about our recovery from the effects of living with the sexaholism of a family member or friend. We do not intend to present a full discussion of the Steps in this book; they are described and explained in depth in the *S-Anon Twelve Steps*, including questions that are meant to help begin the process of working each Step. Here we provide only a brief description of the principles contained in each Step.

1. We admitted we were powerless over sexaholism—that our lives had become unmanageable.

Our numerous and diverse attempts to control or deny sexaholism brought us to the point of despair. We saw that our lives were unmanageable, and we had exhausted our reserves. Only through this utter surrender did we find strength and a firm foundation on which to rebuild our lives. We acknowledged we could not control the sexaholic or his/her sexual behavior and our attempts to do so had made our own lives unmanageable. We learned that our human will alone could not break the bonds of compulsive behavior either in ourselves or others. In S-Anon we came to realize that just as we did not cause the sexaholic's "acting out," we could not cure it either. It was not our responsibility to keep the sexaholic sexually sober. We learned that it was our job to manage our own lives, whether or not the sexaholic chooses recovery. For most of us it was difficult to make the transition from focusing on the sexaholic and his or her behavior to focusing on ourselves and our own behavior. When we admit powerlessness and unmanageability where sexaholism is concerned, we become able to open our minds to the suggestion that positive changes in our lives depend upon changing our own attitudes and behavior, and we become willing to consider accepting help from outside of ourselves in beginning to make those changes.

2. Came to believe that a Power greater than ourselves could restore us to sanity.

We may not have been addicted to sex or substances, but many of us were addicted to people and situations in our lives, and our addiction was just as serious as the sexaholic's addiction to lust. Some of us wondered whether the term "insane" really applied to us, but hadn't we at times acted irrationally within our relationships? Hadn't we often done the same thing over and over again, expecting different results? Step Two suggests that spiritual growth could keep us from repeating unhealthy patterns of behavior. Some of us did not have a problem reaching out to a Higher Power of our understanding. Those of us who did have trouble with the idea of a Higher Power, put our faith in our S-Anon group, listening for the truth spoken through the people and the principles. Once we admitted that we had been unable to solve our problems alone, we became able to ask a Power greater than ourselves for the help we needed.

3. Made a decision to turn our will and our lives over to the care of God *as we understood Him.*

We learned to depend upon a real Higher Power—one with the strength and wisdom to help us in times of need and indecision. Anyone can begin to tap into this source; the key to Step Three was the willingness to allow a Higher Power to take a hand in our lives. Some of us did not have any concept of God when we first came to S-Anon. Some of us had leaned heavily on other people, or tried to please them without regard for our own well-being, in effect making another person (especially the sexaholics in our lives) into a "Higher Power." Many of us were angry or uncomfortable with the concept of God that we had learned early in our lives. But as we shed old ideas that made us feel isolated or unworthy, we began to understand new and hopeful spiritual concepts. We grew in the faith that a loving and caring Higher Power would guide and protect us. Then we were able to make a decision to trust in that care and seek to do God's will instead of our own.

4. Made a searching and fearless moral inventory of ourselves.

Step Four is an action Step. With the loving help of a sponsor and our Higher Power, we took an objective look at our positive and negative attitudes and behavior to see what was really there, and we wrote down what we found. This helped us to recognize and nurture our strengths as well as make changes in some of the ways we thought and acted. For example, we began to see that the sexaholic wasn't the only one causing problems. Although many of us were reluctant to begin this Step for fear of what we would find, as we worked on Step Four most of us began to see that we were neither the worst people nor the best, but somewhere in between, with the rest of the human race. We also found that taking this Step shed light upon aspects of our characters that may have been blocking our spiritual growth.

5. Admitted to God, to ourselves, and to another human being the exact nature of our wrongs.

Step Five might be considered the toughest challenge yet. Just as in Step Four, most of us needed the help of our Higher Power and the support of our sponsor in taking this Step. We first admitted our defects to God, learning to see ourselves and acknowledge what we see to our Higher Power. Then we admitted our shortcomings to ourselves, realizing at a deep level that as human beings we had often made mistakes. Finally, we shared our characteristics, positive and negative, with another trusted human being, emerging from isolation. When we risked sharing our whole story with a supportive person, much of our guilt was relieved and our serenity increased.

6. Were entirely ready to have God remove all these defects of character.

In Step Six we did our best to become ready for God to remove our character defects. We learned that we could not remove our own pride, fear, selfishness, or whatever, with the force of our will, any more than we had been able to force changes in other people. We realized that we needed help from our Higher Power, but God always respects our free will. Nothing could be done until we were willing to live life without the protection we were used to. Most of us have trouble letting go of our defects, because we have used them as our defenses and coping strategies for so long. But we asked God to help us to be willing to give them up, because we wanted to put our trust in a Higher Power, and we saw that our defects stood in our way.

7. Humbly asked him to remove our shortcomings.

Step Seven requires faith. Just as we came to believe in Step Two that a Power greater than ourselves could restore us to sanity, so we came to believe in Step Seven that God could remove our shortcomings. We found that after we took an honest look at our character defects, discussed them with another person, and became willing to have them removed, we experienced a great deal of peace and serenity. When we humbly asked God to remove our shortcomings, even more tranquility came to us. Most of us have found that this Step needs to be taken more than once, but the growth in humility we have experienced in working with Step Seven has served us well, not only when we are asking God for help, but when we are interacting with the people in our lives.

8. Made a list of all persons we had harmed and became willing to make amends to them all.

Step Eight suggested that we begin to "own" our character defects and take responsibility for the choices we made. Many of us were so accustomed to thinking of ourselves as the wronged party that we could not see how we had wronged others. Reviewing our Fourth Step helped us to recognize people we had harmed. In any past relationship, were we attentive, loving, and forgiving, or were we preoccupied, bitter, or resentful? We put all the people we had harmed, including ourselves, on our list. If some of the people on the list had also harmed us, we worked toward forgiveness, recognizing that continuing to blame other sick people would just prolong our misery. When we did not feel willing or able to do this, we asked our Higher Power for help.

9. Made direct amends to such people wherever possible, except when to do so would injure them or others.

We needed discernment, good timing, and courage to take this Step, but with the guidance of God and our sponsor we were able to know whom to approach and when to make amends. We did not wallow in excessive guilt and over responsibility. With the guidance and support of our sponsor and other program members, some of us made amends by going in a forgiving spirit to the person we had harmed and admitting our wrongs with humility. There are other ways of making amends that our sponsor may suggest, but we took the responsibility for doing our part. An important part of Step Nine is "...except when to do so would injure them or others." We must think of the other person (and ourselves) and ask if we will cause more damage. If so, we may find other ways to deal with our feelings and prayerfully consider other options. Working Step Nine was often a positive experience, but even if our amends were not warmly received, our satisfaction and spiritual growth came from acknowledging our wrongs and taking positive action to keep from repeating them.

10. Continued to take personal inventory and when we were wrong promptly admitted it.

In Step Ten we continue to look at our strong and weak points as we let our Higher Power reveal our growth. In the past we rationalized our resentments and allowed them to become the motivation for our actions. We took the same risks with other tempting disturbances like jealousy, envy, self pity, and hurt pride. At these times an inventory of our motives can be of great help in bringing us peace and sanity. We have found the best way to handle our mistakes is to admit we are having difficulty and correct our behavior as soon as possible. This enables us to resolve our conflicts and leave them behind. It keeps our spiritual house, our insides, clean. We can admit our mistakes to God, talk to an S-Anon member, and then offer our amends if need be. The reward is increased acceptance of ourselves and others as struggling human beings.

11. Sought through prayer and meditation to improve our conscious contact with God *as we understood Him*, praying only for knowledge of His will for us and the power to carry that out.

Prayer may be thought of as talking to God, much like talking with a trusted friend. Those of us who have tried it, found that there was power in prayer, even if we were not sure we believed in a Higher Power or had not prayed for a long time. Reaching out to a Higher Power of our understanding has changed our viewpoint and allowed us to see ourselves and our problems in different and helpful ways.

To meditate means to ponder or reflect. It is a time when we can be quiet with God and within ourselves. We hope to be inspired toward new understanding of God's will for us, and we let our innermost selves be receptive to new ideas for our growth. Regular practice of this Step has rewarded us with emotional balance and a sense of belonging and peace.

12. Having had a spiritual awakening as the result of these Steps, we tried to carry this message to others, and to practice these principles in all our affairs.

For most of us a spiritual awakening has been a gradual process—through practicing the Twelve Steps we found ourselves experiencing a degree of honesty, tolerance, unselfishness, serenity, and love which seemed impossible before recovery. One definition of a spiritual awakening is the ability to do, feel, and believe, through God's power, that which a person could not do before with his or her own power. We have awakened to a concept of a loving God in our lives. We truly have been changed.

We try to carry the S-Anon message by sharing our experience, strength, and hope with others, and we have found our joy and gratitude growing when we see the attitudes of other women and men change from despair to hope. We have seen that we can be uniquely helpful to those who are still suffering from the effects of sexaholism. We also strive to bring the same love and tolerance we are developing in our S-Anon group and in our close family relationships into our other personal, work, and community relationships. We have found this to be the path toward continued spiritual growth.

OBSERVING THE TWELVE TRADITIONS
OF S-ANON

S-Anon's Twelve Traditions are principles that guide the conduct and unity of our groups. The Traditions guide the growth and health of our groups and our world wide fellowship, just as the Twelve Steps guide our growth and our lives as individual members. The Traditions evolved from the experience of AA and Al-Anon groups in solving their problems of living and working together. S-Anon adapted these Traditions as group guidelines, and over the years members of our fellowship have found them to be sound and wise. Without healthy groups, there would be very little individual recovery. As we grow in our understanding of the Traditions, we also find that applying these principles to other areas of our lives can guide us toward healthier relationships with family, friends, co-workers, and others.

This section contains brief and general summaries of how the main ideas and principles underlying each of the Twelve Traditions apply to both our S-Anon groups and, in many cases, our families. Each time we read the Traditions in a meeting, we are reminded that "our group experience suggests that the unity of the S-Anon Family Groups depends upon our adherence to the following Traditions:"

1. Our common welfare should come first; personal progress for the greatest number depends upon unity.

Tradition One asks us to recognize that the needs or desires of one individual, or even one group, do not take precedence over the need for the S-Anon Fellowship to maintain unity of purpose and message. Thus, Tradition One guides us toward maintaining enough continuity within our groups that no matter which S-Anon meeting we attend, we will feel at home because many of the elements will be similar. Our S-Anon Conference Approved Literature (CAL) is the written material that conveys S-Anon's unified message of experience, strength, and hope to each group and individual member, so we use only CAL at our meetings to maintain our unity. Tradition One also reminds us that all members benefit by both listening and sharing at a meeting. Repeated, prolonged sharing by any individual, no matter how much they may "need to express themselves," is contrary to the welfare of the group. At another level, we can turn to the wisdom of this Tradition when thinking about or discussing issues related to unity within our families or in our workplaces. That is, we do well to consider the needs of the family, our coworkers or the S-Anon group as a whole, as well as our individual needs and desires, when making decisions or taking actions.

2. For our group purpose there is but one authority—a loving God as he may express Himself in our group conscience. Our leaders are but trusted servants, they do not govern.

Through working the first three Steps, we saw the benefit of turning our individual lives over to the care of God. Tradition Two teaches us how to use the same process to work out problems or make decisions in our groups and families. A decision that is discussed thoroughly by as many members as possible and is guided by a Higher Power is an expression of the group conscience. In Al-Anon literature we find this comforting guideline: "When we all seek God's will, there can be no winning or losing, but only a journey to greater understanding." [4] It is important to note that it is possible that a decision taken by group conscience may, as time passes, need to be reconsidered. We are always free to take a fresh look at a decision made in the past if it seems that the results of that decision are not what we had hoped. Leadership positions do exist within the local and regional groups and the worldwide fellowship, but members rotate in and out of leadership positions. The leaders are assuming responsibility, not authority. We can practice Tradition Two with our family members by praying for guidance from our Higher Power before discussing family problems. We can also remind ourselves that even those in positions of authority in a family—the parents—do not always have all the answers. Spiritual principles are often expressed clearly by even the youngest members of a family.

---

[4] *Al-Anon Paths to Recovery*, p. 146

3. The relatives of sexaholics, when gathered together for mutual aid, may call themselves an S-Anon Family Group, provided that, as a group, they have no other affiliation. The only requirement for membership is that there be a problem of sexaholism in a relative or friend.

The Third Tradition assures S-Anon's singleness of purpose. Anyone whose life has been affected by a sexaholic relative or friend "qualifies" to join S-Anon. Some areas provide a local phone number for newcomers, so that they have an opportunity speak to a program member before attending their first meeting, but this should not be thought of as a screening process. Individuals qualify for S-Anon as soon as they say they do. We do not exclude anyone, even if his or her relationship with a sexaholic does not match our own. It does not matter which, if any, Twelve Step recovery program his or her sexaholic family member or friend may or may not be working. The spiritual principle in Tradition Three asks us to maintain a sense of belonging and equality for everyone. We do not make references to specific religious denominations, professions, or other affiliations during our meetings. Likewise, we do not affiliate an individual group with the church or hospital where the meeting is being held. For many of us, our S-Anon group was the first place we felt we really belonged. Tradition Three reminds us to strive to maintain an atmosphere in which everyone who needs the help of S-Anon feels welcome. An S-Anon group, by the definition of Tradition Three, is open to any individual who identifies a problem of sexaholism in a family member or friend.

A local area may decide to hold a special meeting for certain members, such as, for men or parents or couples, which is distinct from a regular S-Anon group. See the *S-Anon/S-Ateen Service Manual* (Part 1 and Appendix D) for more information.

4. Each group should be autonomous, except in matters affecting another group or S-Anon or SA as a whole.

Tradition Four reminds us to consider how the actions of our group may affect others as we participate in meetings and other S-Anon activities. Each group has autonomy in matters such as deciding what time the meeting starts and ends, adding special newcomer meetings, or choosing a closing prayer (such as the Serenity Prayer or Third Step Prayer). On the other hand, bringing outside literature into the meeting, adding outside readings to the meeting format or changing the wording of Conference Approved Literature are examples of matters that would affect S-Anon as a whole. The S-Anon Fellowship as a whole would be affected because, by Fellowship-wide group conscience, we limit the use of literature in our meetings to S-Anon Conference Approved Literature (that is, literature approved by the Fellowship as a whole). This assures that the focus in our meetings remains on S-Anon principles. (The S-Anon/S-Ateen Literature Conference Approval Process may be found in the *S-Anon/S-Ateen Service Manual*.) Likewise, when we participate in planning S-Anon events such as conventions, weekend gatherings, or marathons, we recognize that we conduct these activities on behalf of S-Anon at the regional or national level, and we are thus bound to consider the guidelines that are the result of the experiences of other S-Anon groups who have planned such events. Tradition Four can also guide our family relationships as we consider that each partner or adult family member should be autonomous, except in matters affecting the other partner, the family, or society as a whole.

5. Each S-Anon Family Group has but one purpose: to help families of sexaholics. We do this by practicing the Twelve Steps of S-Anon, by encouraging and understanding our sexaholic relatives, and by welcoming and giving comfort to the families of sexaholics.

This Tradition clearly states that the reason S-Anon exists as a fellowship is to help the families of sexaholics. Long before we came into S-Anon, most of us had plenty of experience with helping others, but Tradition Five suggests that we need to be practicing the Twelve Steps of S-Anon ourselves if we are to be of service to others in a healthy way. When we first come to S-Anon, the idea of "encouraging and understanding our sexaholic relatives" may be confusing to us. Most of us felt hurt and angry at the sexaholic. Through working the Twelve Steps and sharing with others, we begin to see sexaholism as a disease, develop compassion for the sexaholic, and learn to detach with love. We can also welcome and give comfort to other S-Anon members even when they are different from us or when they share a story that may evoke strong emotions in us. Tradition Five can be very helpful in our families and other relationships. It reminds us that rather than trying to solve the problems of others, often we can help them most by practicing the principles of S-Anon to the best of our ability, while at the same time offering our encouragement and understanding.

6. Our S-Anon Family Groups ought never endorse, finance, or lend our name to any outside enterprise, lest problems of money, property, and prestige divert us from our primary spiritual aim. Although a separate entity, we should always cooperate with Sexaholics Anonymous.

S-Anon is a spiritual program, not a religious program. S-Anon is open to those of all religions and also to those with no religious participation. Therefore, to keep the focus on our common purpose rather than on individual differences, in our meetings we use general terms such as "God," "God of my understanding," or "Higher Power" and we avoid references to specific religious denominations. Similarly, many S-Anon members and sexaholics have been helped by professional therapists, but S-Anon cannot assume the responsibility of recommending them. If we mentioned names of therapists, treatment centers, or self-help books in our meetings or advertised them in S-Anon publications, we would seem to be endorsing them and associating the S-Anon name with them, potentially distracting us from our primary spiritual aim. An S-Anon meeting is not a place to sell any particular product, or discuss any particular philosophy, religion, or therapy. It is also important to note that S-Anon International Family Groups and Sexaholics Anonymous (SA) are two separate and very different fellowships. They are independent of one another. S-Anon may cooperate, however, with the SA Fellowship for specific events. An example is an S-Anon planning committee cooperating with SA committee members in coordinating a Regional or International Convention. Also, S-Anon groups may have a local contact information telephone line, which is answered by S-Anon members, but the cost of the line is shared with SA. The remote line will actually house both the S-Anon contact phone number and the SA contact phone number, but will receive one billing statement.

7. Every group ought to be fully self-supporting, declining outside contributions.

The S-Anon World Service Office, regional intergroups and our local S-Anon groups are entirely supported by the financial and service contributions of S-Anon members, and we are bound by this Tradition to assume our freely chosen financial obligations as a fellowship. This includes paying rent for our meeting space and declining offers to use meeting space for free. It is also suggested that each registered S-Anon group send in a monthly financial contribution to the S-Anon World Service Office. Our World Service Office relies on financial donations from groups and individual members, and upon sale of S-Anon literature to pay office employees, print literature, and to maintain communication with the worldwide Fellowship and the professional community. "Fully self-supporting" can, however, refer to more than just financial support. Each member of the group has an opportunity to support the group by taking a turn in a service position, such as chairing a meeting, answering or returning local contact calls, leading newcomer meetings, or volunteering at a convention or open meeting. Similarly, each member of a family can be encouraged to strive to be physically, emotionally, and spiritually self-supporting to an appropriate extent.

8. S-Anon Twelfth Step work should remain forever non-professional, but our service centers may employ special workers.

S-Anon members are never paid for their Twelfth Step work, that is, for carrying the message of their own recovery to others. In this regard, while professionals such as physicians, counselors, and clergy sometimes come to S-Anon meetings for their own recovery, when speaking at a meeting, marathon, or convention, they do so as members of S-Anon only, not as professionals in their field. Special workers are employees of S-Anon who take care of our World Service Office work, fill literature orders, respond to requests for information, and maintain financial records. We believe it is our responsibility as a fellowship to pay these special workers a reasonable rate for their work. These employees may or may not be S-Anon members. S-Anon members who do not work at the S-Anon International Family Groups (SAIFG) World Service Office may also be paid by SAIFG or an Area Office for using their specialized skills (such as administrative, accounting, website management, clerical, editing, or writing skills) on behalf of S-Anon. Employing special workers keeps us in line with the Seventh Tradition as well —our fellowship is self-supporting when we pay for services we receive.

9. Our groups, as such, ought never be organized, but we may create service boards or committees directly responsible to those they serve.

Sometimes newcomers are amazed that S-Anon has no formal organization. There is no president or executive that governs the fellowship and enforces rules. But we have found that we need some degree of organization. If everybody thinks somebody is going to order the literature, what's the result? No literature gets ordered! In all cases, however, those who take part in S-Anon service work are assuming responsibility – not authority. Each group sets up its own service structure, and S-Anon groups operate according to suggestions and principles found in these Twelve Traditions. Most groups have a treasurer, but the treasurer does not collect "dues" and cannot compel anyone to pay anything. Occasionally, a member who starts a meeting may feel that he or she "owns" or is personally responsible for the success of the meeting. This is not helpful to the individual or to the group. To help prevent this situation it is important that meetings are held in a neutral location, service positions are rotated, and business meetings are held on a regular basis to discuss group issues. S-Anon does have a very simple service structure that operates at a fellowship-wide level; the S-Anon Board of Trustees meets by conference call monthly to discuss matters affecting the fellowship as a whole. (Additional information on the S-Anon service structure may be found in the *S-Anon/S-Ateen Service Manual.*)

10. The S-Anon Family Groups have no opinions on outside issues, hence our name ought never be drawn into public controversy.

Discussion of outside issues, especially in the context of an S-Anon meeting, can divert us from our primary spiritual aim—helping family members and friends of sexaholics. For example, there are many anti-pornography groups in existence, and much time could be spent deciding which ones S-Anon should support. This time-consuming process would keep us from focusing on carrying the message of our own recovery and possible differences of opinion could detract from the unity we seek in our groups. As individuals, we can become involved or express our opinion on any issue. We do not, however, offer our opinions on social, political, or religious issues as S-Anon members. Likewise, each member of a family or work group is entitled to his or her opinion. If family or work group members have widely divergent views on particular political issues, for example, it may be best to avoid this controversial topic, if it seems to detract from family or group unity, and "agree to disagree."

11. Our public relations policy is based on attraction rather than promotion; we need always maintain personal anonymity at the level of press, radio, TV, and films. We need guard with special care the anonymity of all S-Anon and SA members.

Anonymity assures S-Anon members and newcomers to our program that meetings are safe places. We are free to share our full names, professions, and other identifying information with others, but in meetings and when speaking as S-Anon members to the public, we avoid mentioning our professional titles, and we usually introduce ourselves by first names only. If we appear in the media as S-Anon members, we do so in such a way that we remain anonymous (that is, using first names only, faced away from the camera, etc.). If we choose to break our own personal anonymity by using our full names, we need to take care not to break the anonymity of a Sexaholics Anonymous member without that member's permission. This does not mean we must continue to keep secrets, but we do respect others to the highest degree possible. For example, when sharing in a meeting or telling our story, we usually do not refer to the sexaholic or to another S-Anon member by name. The principle of anonymity also dictates that the personal information we hear from other members during meetings, phone calls, emails, or other contacts should not be repeated to others. This includes keeping names and stories in confidence, even when talking with spouses and other family members, and taking care to keep contact information of members in a safe, private place. We do not "promote" the S-Anon Program in the usual sense of that word. We often find that family members or friends who may need the help of S-Anon are more likely to be attracted by our changed attitudes and actions than by long explanations of how the program works or extended testimonials, no matter how well-intentioned.

12. Anonymity is the spiritual foundation of all our Traditions, ever reminding us to place principles above personalities.

Our Twelfth Tradition teaches us the value of humility. In S-Anon, our family background, where we live or what we do for a living is not important. By maintaining anonymity, we are practicing humility in our recovery. For example, disagreements are bound to come up from time to time within a group because we all come from different backgrounds and have different personalities. Focusing on the principles of the Twelve Traditions when discussing group issues helps us to respect each other and to work together in harmony. The spirit of anonymity is carried throughout our Conference Approved Literature. Individual members are not given special recognition as authors of particular pieces of literature, and members are not mentioned by name when personal stories are published. Placing principles before personalities in our families also can bring rich rewards. We can remind ourselves that even those in position of authority in a family do not necessarily have all the answers. The principle of "Anonymity" is very important to S-Anon members and a separate section of this book has been devoted to it beginning on page 43.

DEPENDING ON A HIGHER POWER

In S-Anon we define Higher Power as "a Power greater than our-selves." When we accepted our inability to solve our problems on our own, we became open to the idea of a Higher Power. As we let our Higher Power work in our lives, we were amazed at the changes that became possible, and we found a new freedom. Our Higher Power is the God of our own understanding, not someone else's understanding. We were encouraged to think about our own thoughts, feelings, and conception of God and to grow in our understanding from there. For some people their group has even served as their Higher Power. We have found that our understanding of God did not have to be set, but was changing and growing with us. To provide safety for all in our meetings, we do not talk about our specific religious beliefs or literature so that we are not diverted from our primary purpose. We do not judge anyone's understanding of God, and we do not try to impose our beliefs on other members. Rather, we talk about our personal Higher Power and do not expect others to have the same point of view.

●   ●   ●

MEMBERS SHARE

Smiling Again... I give the credit to my Higher Power for lifting my bitterness and resentment. I'm not sure when it happened, and I know I didn't plan it. I thought I had good reason to be angry for the rest of my life, but found that I am not hurting inside anymore. I have hope, and I can laugh again. It is a miracle.

As We Understood... When I first came to S-Anon, I was inwardly critical of others' references to God when they didn't match my own. I was also uncomfortable with all the references to "He" in the Steps. As I really started to work the program, many of these issues faded. I came to "Live and Let Live," and asked myself "How important is it?" I found that I could have my understanding and accepted that others could have theirs.

New Levels... When I came to S-Anon, I thought I had already done Steps One, Two, and Three, because I already believed in a loving God and had given my life to Him. As I learned more about the Steps, I realized that I had a very hard time admitting my powerlessness and turning over to God certain situations in my life. I had been sure that if I were just good enough, smart enough, or had tried long enough and hard enough, things would turn out O.K.—or the way I wanted. I had to learn and continue to learn that I do not have power over sexaholism, that the sexaholic in my life has a Higher Power, too, and that God is the only one who can restore me to sanity and serenity.

Hoping in a Higher Power... The only solution to my fear, my desire to control, and my feelings of victimization has been to live one minute at a time and to act as if I trust God, even when I don't. I look back on all my losses, and even though I see that each one in the end turned out to be best for me, I still feel angry and fearful. But I do know one thing for sure: I am not God. This small amount of humility allows me to know that I do not know what is best for me, or for anyone else. I have seen that things I thought were best were not, and, as a result, I am beginning to see that my self-righteousness is not based on reality. This gives me the hope that God does know what is best for me. I know that I cannot get my partner sober or save our relationship, only God can. I must let go of trying to control, and let God do whatever he is going to do, even if I don't want to. I don't know if that is willingness, but it is all I have.

A Real Higher Power... In my life before recovery, many people I considered to be "powers greater than myself" abused me with that power emotionally, physically, sexually, and spiritually. As a result, when I came to S-Anon I was not eager to willingly "turn myself over" to any power. Building on the foundation of Step Two, I have begun to experience a true spiritual connection with a Power greater than myself and have become willing to turn my will and my life over to that Power. I have begun to trust in the experiences of others and have surrendered my need to control every situation to protect myself from nameless, faceless, countless dangers. I have seen that this Power can be trusted, will always be with me, and will never abandon or betray me. This does not mean that my life will be free of difficulties – it does mean that I will have what I need to face them and will not have to face them alone.

Quiet Time... It's so hard for me to sit down for some quiet time with my Higher Power. I know an uncontrollable fear is at the root of this. I fear the challenges that I must face if I am honest with myself. So here I sit with all my fears. I feel a gentle tugging to stay in the quiet and let it do its work. Why do I resist? My Higher Power has given me this precious time alone. I need to get in touch with what's going on with me (and only me) for today. I don't want to, but I do need to. It's time to leave any expectations at the door. Any expectations of suffocating fears or of being swept away in my self-defeating thinking must be put aside. I don't even expect to get a clear, immediate message from my Higher Power. For now, it's time to let go of each little thing that crowds me, even if it means letting go for just a minute at a time. In this quiet it is just me and my Higher Power. It is in this silence that I realize how little I really do know. Maybe that's the best place to start. Humble beginnings. I pray I can be open to whatever comes my way in the quiet. I ask God to help me loosen my grip. I ask Him to help me open up to His will for me. I know I am not alone now.

USING THE SERENITY PRAYER

God, grant me the serenity
To accept the things I cannot change,
Courage to change the things I can,
And wisdom to know the difference.

The Serenity Prayer is said as an opening and/or closing at most group meetings. Sometimes it is used as a topic for group discussion, and it inspires many of us in our daily meditations. The Serenity Prayer reminds us that we do not have the power to change other people, things, or outside circumstances. Rather, it suggests that we do have the ability to make positive changes in our own behaviors and attitudes. The Serenity Prayer points out that our Higher Power guides us in our recovery process and that powerlessness is not the same as helplessness. In fact, we have found we are most able to be helped when we realize that our power is limited and we really need help.

•   •   •

MEMBERS SHARE

Relief... In the beginning, I said the Serenity Prayer a lot to help me learn that some things were in my power to control and some were not. At the time, I was extremely frustrated because I didn't like the choices my sexaholic husband was making about his job, and I couldn't get my two-year-old to do the things I wanted him to do. The Serenity Prayer helped me get through that difficult time. Today, this prayer continues to help me breathe better and lighten up a little. I know today I can't make my son go to sleep, like vegetables, or have a good relationship with his dad. However, I can create a calm atmosphere and set limits about what time he has to be in bed. I can also speak to my spouse about my needs and wants.

Restored to Sanity... About six months after I began working the S-Anon Program, my denial came crashing down on me and my long-suppressed feelings came bubbling up. I felt overwhelmed. I used one of the few tools that I had at that point (and one that came readily to mind): I said the Serenity Prayer over and over again until the overwhelming feelings passed. It worked; it restored me to sanity and continued to do so as I worked through those painful feelings. I'm grateful for the simplicity of this prayer.

Living the Serenity Prayer... The Serenity Prayer helps me realize the difference between my responsibility and the other person's responsibility. It involves taking control of me and letting go of my control of others' actions and opinions. That's easier said than done, though, and I've had to work at finding ways to make this prayer a reality in my life.

Accepting Things I Cannot Change... Accepting the past as past has become important to my serenity. I have faced my past and called it what it is. Thankfully, it does not need to be repeated, nor does it need to remain so hurtful to me. I can give up my past dreams and idealistic goals. I can make new goals that include myself and my Higher Power's will for me.

Courage to Change the Things I Can... I am learning to trust myself to rise to the occasion as a problem presents itself. I will have the resources when I need them. I don't have to control the outcome, but can learn to trust the process. This allows me to be less afraid of the future. I am learning to accept change and not automatically see it as the end of the world or negative, but rather an opportunity for growth.

The Wisdom to Know the Difference... I am learning to distinguish between what I can do and what's not my responsibility. I can take responsibility for myself and stop my own negative behaviors. I can identify those things I find difficult to accept that cause me physical, emotional, or spiritual depletion. I can choose to take care of myself by spending quality time with God. The more I get to know God, the more I trust His love and care for me.

RESPECTING ANONYMITY

The principle of "anonymity" in S-Anon operates at several different levels. First, anonymity protects us as individuals, our fellowship as a whole, and our sexaholic family members or friends from public exposure and gossip. We never reveal a person's name, association with the program, or confidences anyone has shared. Anonymity as referred to in Traditions Eleven and Twelve also helps us place principles above personalities. We are all equal in the S-Anon Fellowship—our outside status and position make no difference. At fellowship gatherings and conventions we practice this principle by listing topics, rather than individual speakers, on flyers and programs. S-Anon is a fellowship of equals—there are no VIPs or "stars." Finally, at the level of press, radio, film, television, and other public communications, we do not allow our last names or our faces to be revealed if we identify ourselves as S-Anon members. We do not want to risk giving the impression that any one person speaks for S-Anon.

• • •

MEMBERS SHARE

Liberated... Going to an S-Anon meeting was a major step for me. My husband was a minister and a practicing sexaholic. I felt extremely ashamed to be subjected to the whole thing. My family knew nothing about it, nor did our church. It was very important to me at that time to keep it that way. It took a long time for me to trust this thing called anonymity. When I finally told my group my fears and my agony of having shameful secrets, I felt liberated. My meeting became one place where I did not feel paralyzed by fear of other people's expectations and impressions of me or my family.

Examining my Motives... I have discovered that I sometimes disclose my affiliation with S-Anon too easily. For example, I tell someone I go to S-Anon in order to defend the Twelve Steps. I think it would be helpful for me to be more discerning of my motives before I talk about my membership in S-Anon. I can talk about S-

Anon when it seems appropriate or I can offer information or a pamphlet about the program without revealing my association with the fellowship.

A New Concept... Tradition Twelve states "Anonymity is the spiritual foundation of all our Traditions, ever reminding us to place principles above personalities." The equality implied by "principles above personalities" was the opposite of the dynamic with which I grew up. I had learned not to say things that might upset someone and to adjust myself to the personality at hand—I was funny, sarcastic, angry, or quiet—I played them all very well. So to follow this aspect of anonymity was difficult but important for me to learn.

Anonymity and Trust... I work an S-Anon Program as well as a sexaholic recovery program, and I go to a number of meetings in the area. One day while talking to an S-Anon member, she admitted she and her husband (who attends my other program) had discussed what I had said at a meeting. I was devastated that my anonymity had been broken and that this person justified her behavior as "necessary" to ensure that her husband was not somehow acting out in the meeting or with program people. I just know that for me to obtain serenity, I have to do recovery in double-time. I need to take my recovery pulse and go to the meeting that is appropriate, but these events seemed to just confirm my sick belief that I should trust no one. I once again have had to learn forgiveness toward people who have hurt me, and realize again that I cannot control other people or outcomes. I have also had to continue to work a strong recovery program despite my trust issues. The importance of respecting everyone's anonymity regarding what is shared in meetings cannot be overstated, from my point of view.

DEVELOPING NEW ATTITUDES

KEEPING THE FOCUS ON OURSELVES

As we have heard many times in the program, "We didn't cause the addiction, we cannot control it, and we cannot cure it." How difficult it is to accept that others can help sexaholics in recovery when we cannot. "It takes one to know one" is a saying that sums up the wisdom contained in the suggestion that one addict can best help another addict, but because we have so often felt like victims, our ability to see sexaholics objectively is usually very limited. We have often spent years trying to control other people's behavior. If we bring that behavior into recovery, especially at first when we know very little about how to work the Twelve Steps in our own lives, it can only lead to more frustration. The way out of this frustration is to begin to put the focus on ourselves and our own actions and reactions.

> In S-Anon we come to realize that just as we did not cause the sexaholic's acting out, we cannot 'cure' it either. We learn that it is not our responsibility to keep the sexaholic sexually sober. Instead, it is our job to manage our own lives, whether or not the sexaholic chooses sobriety. [5]

● ● ●

MEMBERS SHARE

"...we cannot cure it."... "I wonder if I'm really a sexaholic," said my husband one day after about a year in recovery. "Maybe I really don't need those meetings and the program." Panic overwhelmed me, and in my mind's eye I could see nothing but a black future. I imagined my husband going back "out there" to have another affair (or two or three), leaving our marriage in shambles.

---

[5] *S-Anon Twelve Steps*, p. 2

My first instinct was to try to convince him that he really was a sex-aholic. I began to mentally list all the hurtful things he had done in the past which proved (to me!) that he was powerless over his sex-ual behavior, and I was about to remind him of each and every event in case he had forgotten.

But I, too, had been in recovery for a year, and I remembered all the times we had talked in meetings about "letting go and letting God." A little inner voice told me this was a time to let go. So I said nothing, just nodded to let him know I had been listening. I hoped he wouldn't notice how afraid and upset I was. A little while later my husband said, "I've been thinking about it, and I guess I am a sexaholic. I think I'll go to a meeting tonight." As I reflected on how things worked out, I became aware that my husband must have resented my past efforts to control his thinking, and felt even more need to defend himself and his ideas. Instead, because I kept quiet, this time we were both able to think things through in a calm atmosphere.

Do I Really Know What Is Best?... I have heard people say that working the program is like taking a shower—no one can do it for you. So when I feel the need to "help" or try to make things turn out the way I think they should, I may be standing in the way of both my partner's and my recovery without realizing it. I have a hard time not giving my opinion because he used to ask me time and again "What do you think?" and "What should I do?" Now I am aware that if I feel a decision he's trying to make might affect me in some way, it is rarely possible for me to be objective. It is actually a load off my mind when I accept that no matter how much I love my husband, I cannot be certain what is best for him. In fact, I must admit that I often do not know what is best for myself!

I Can Only Change Myself... I always thought that when my husband had sobriety things would be better. Now that he is sober and things are not better, I'm left looking at myself, and I'm finding that it's harder than looking at him! I keep thinking "Is this all there is? Is this what life is about?" But I think there's more to recovery than I have experienced so far, and part of me knows what I need to do. Maybe I am uncomfortable because my prayers haven't been answered the way I wanted them to be —"make my life better by fixing him." I have prayed for help, but maybe the answer is that I need to make changes in my own life.

I Must Stop Playing God in My Partner's Life... When I feel the urge to try to be my husband's "sponsor," I know I need to do two things. First, I can put one of the S-Anon slogans into practice, and "keep the focus on myself." I can ask myself questions like: "Does this situation make me feel afraid of abandonment? If so, why? Am I afraid to trust the program? Do I secretly feel superior to my spouse, believing that he cannot function without my "help"? My own road to recovery has been based upon the answers to questions like these, not upon the actions or feelings of my husband. The second thing I can do is realize that for my own good, I must stop playing God in my partner's life. I can learn to trust that the life and recovery of my spouse is also in the care of a "power greater than myself." If I have come to believe that a Higher Power can restore me to sanity, I can trust that the same is true for my partner.

INCREASING OUR HONESTY, OPEN-MINDEDNESS, AND WILLINGNESS

B eginning on page 567 of the *Big Book of Alcoholics Anonymous* (Fourth Edition), the requirements for having a "spiritual experience" were clarified to correct the mistaken impression that a spiritual experience or spiritual awakening was always sudden and spectacular in nature or that a total "God consciousness" must necessarily be acquired before progress can be made in the Twelve Step program. It is a comforting section, in which we are reassured that progress toward increased spirituality and awareness of a Higher Power can be made gradually:

> Most emphatically we wish to say that any alcoholic capable of honestly facing his problems in the light of our experience can recover, provided he does not close his mind to all spiritual concepts. He can only be defeated by an attitude of intolerance or belligerent denial. We find that no one need have difficulty with the spirituality of the program. *Willingness, honesty and open mindedness are the essentials of recovery. But these are indispensable.*[6]

These three essential components, Honesty, Open Mindedness, and Willingness, are often referred to as the "HOW," in "HOW the program works." This shorthand has been adopted by other Twelve Step programs, including S-Anon, to indicate our commitment to growth in these fundamental qualities.

HONESTY

Honesty is commitment to the truth. In our spiritual illness, many of us convinced ourselves that things were not the way they seemed. We lied to ourselves, our partners, and others—sometimes without even realizing it. This state of mind is sometimes called "being in denial." In recovery we are invited to move out of denial and face reality. At first this felt scary and painful. Some of us feared

---

[6]*Alcoholics Anonymous*, Fourth Edition, p. 568

the consequences of facing the truth. Learning to listen to our hearts and to honor our feelings takes time and work. Some of us felt confused for a while and unsure if our perceptions were valid. We learned the value of reaching out and getting "reality checks" from others in the program. In time, we learned to recognize the truth ourselves and to accept reality.

• • •

MEMBERS SHARE

Letting Others See Me... The struggle to be honest brings me face-to-face with the "old tools" that have been with me since childhood. My first instinct is to fit in—agree with others—and if I don't, keep it to myself. Fear of my father's anger caused me to keep such a tight rein on my feelings and opinions that in time I lost sight of what my feelings and opinions were. There seemed to be no me! As I connect at deeper levels with my Higher Power's love for me, I feel a greater ability to be honest, to know myself, and to let myself be seen and heard by others. The boat may rock, but I haven't sunk yet!

Developing Honesty... Working with my sponsor has helped me develop my commitment to honesty. She not only models living an honest life, she also gently confronts me about my faulty thinking and other areas where I'm not yet totally honest with myself and others.

Awareness... I have always tried to be honest. For example, I didn't think that I was an angry person and I might have said that I was not angry. Yet in recovery, I learned that I did have a lot of anger and resentments, which I wasn't able to see before. As awareness came, I learned to identify my feelings and to talk about them. I became more honest with myself and others and learned to deal with my anger more appropriately.

Honesty or HONESTY?... Are there two types of honesty? For me, there seem to be. First is the ego boosting kind where I look like such an honest person. For example, I may have returned something given to me by mistake or corrected a clerk who gave me too much change. This type of honesty is important, but compared to the second type, it's easy because I will usually get a lot of approval and others are so pleased. HONESTY of the second type is much harder for me because I must own a wrong I have done or a character defect. HONESTY brings me to my knees with humility. In the fellowship of S-Anon I have been finding the love and support to work on this more difficult, yet rewarding form of HONESTY. It is like a "breath of fresh air" as the weight and pain of dishonest secrets are acknowledged. With the first type of honesty I can be relatively sure that others will respond in a positive fashion. Since one of my character defects is to try to control things, this honesty is easier for me. It seems risky when I venture out with the second type of HONESTY. Others could respond by rejecting me or being hurt or angry—emotions I prefer to avoid in my life as I try to protect myself. Thanks to the trust I am developing with my fellow S-Anon members, I am being more HONEST and finding warmth and loving acceptance. What a wonderful gift! I continue to be grateful for what I have been given.

OPEN-MINDEDNESS

Open-mindedness is being receptive to new ideas. It was hard for many of us to accept the idea that we were not as open-minded as we thought we were. Our set ways of seeing things made us sure we could show others a few things about life. To begin to see our rigid, judgmental, and self-righteous attitudes was painful for most of us. Sometimes fear made letting go of our rigid ideas especially difficult. Yet we found truth in the saying, "nothing changes if nothing changes." Hungry for recovery, we gradually began to identify and surrender our urges to say "Yes, but..." We began to open ourselves to the possibility that the experiences of others working the S-Anon Program could be applied to our own lives. As we progress in our own recovery, we lose our grandiosity and gain a richness of life beyond anything we could have imagined possible.

• • •

MEMBERS SHARE

Simple Solutions... At one of my first meetings, "slogans" was the topic of discussion. I smugly thought, "I can't believe they really use these cliches." My academic values had taught me to think that life's problems had to be solved by complex solutions from deep thinkers. But the more I came to meetings and began working the S-Anon Program, the more I saw the real wisdom in the simple sayings. "Act as if..." and "Keep It Simple" are surprisingly practical and helped me through difficult, emotionally-draining situations.

Accepting Help... I think my Higher Power is opening my mind to accept help in whatever way He chooses to provide it. I used to think that I shouldn't need to talk to a counselor. I thought my faith in God and prayer would get me through, but I eventually learned that accepting help from a trained counselor was helpful to me. Then I said, "I shouldn't need to go to those Twelve Step groups." Wrong again. S-Anon has helped me immensely. More recently I thought, "I shouldn't need that kind of medication." Again I was wrong. I think I have opened my mind enough to admit that I don't know everything. While these forms of help may not be for everyone in S-Anon, being open-minded allowed me to choose to accept the help I needed.

Allowing God to Work... I thought I had an open mind because I could listen to people and understand them. I thought I understood my sexaholic relatives and knew what they needed. My intentions were not bad, but I started to see that I was not always right. My efforts were interfering with God's timing and His dealing with the sexaholic and other people. I was humbled, knowing I was not the Higher Power and that my perspective was limited. My mind was opened to a much bigger Higher Power that was working in my life and the lives of others.

WILLINGNESS

Willingness is the readiness to take positive action. Most of us first demonstrate willingness to recover when we come to an S-Anon meeting. It becomes clear that when we are "sick and tired of being sick and tired" and in pain, we are ready to do whatever it takes. It becomes clear that without on-going willingness, spiritual growth is not possible. We show our willingness by going to meetings, sharing at meetings, making telephone calls, working the Steps, learning the Traditions, doing service, and thoughtfully considering suggestions from our sponsors. "Willingness" continues to challenge us as we make progress in our recovery—when we speak to a newcomer, sponsor someone, apply the suggestions of a sponsor, and do Step work. Willingness is an attitude that stems from humility—how teachable we are. Many of us experience increased willingness when we ask our Higher Power for it. Willingness moves us toward the promised gifts of the S-Anon Program, which include serenity, dignity, and emotional growth.

● ● ●

MEMBERS SHARE

Walking through Fear... What generally stands between me and willingness is fear. I'm usually willing to do things that feel comfortable to me, but when I'm afraid, my willingness diminishes. For example, when I was first asked to lead a meeting, I fearfully said "no." But the person asking encouraged me by saying that we were all equals and that we all supported the group. Her words helped me become willing. Now when fear comes up—whether it's working with a sponsee or setting a boundary with the sexaholic, I ask my Higher Power to be with me and to increase my willingness to walk through my fear.

New Meaning ... For me, when I came to S-Anon I was "willing" to do anything for just about anybody. The kind of willingness I had to learn was willingness to set boundaries or limits—where to draw the line. I had to say "no" and become willing to make room for another voice, my Higher Power, who would tell me He loved me, and I didn't have to do anything for it—just be willing to receive it.

Just Willing... Step Six speaks to me about willingness. Understanding that Step Six is not an "action" step brought about a mini-spiritual awakening for me. For most of my life, I was trying to heal my being by doing. Working on Step Six gave me the confidence that all I needed was willingness. I didn't have to remove the character defects myself. I just needed to identify my shortcomings and be willing to allow God to remove these defects in His time and in His way.

Willing to go to Any Length... When I find myself falling into "Yes, but..." thinking, I try to listen to an S-Anon Convention tape I have about being willing to go to any length. One of the speakers on this tape talks about being willing to go to any length for his recovery, just like he had been for his disease. Another speaker talks about being willing to drive three hours—one way, across an international border even—to go to an S-Anon meeting every week for the better part of a year until she could start a meeting in her area. Hearing about willingness like that puts my own situation into better perspective.

DEFINING OUR EMOTIONAL SOBRIETY

We find that each of us has particular behaviors and attitudes that we have found to be destructive to ourselves and that we hope to eliminate, thus becoming more "sober." Some of us wanted to let go of behaviors like snooping, raging at the sexaholic, or lying to family and friends to cover up the addiction, for example. Others wanted to become more honest with ourselves and others or to become more tolerant and open minded. We have used individual strategies for changing these actions and attitudes, as we must if we wish to find serenity. However, all of us have failed in our efforts from time to time and found ourselves repeating the destructive behavior almost before we knew it. In S-Anon, we often call this a relapse, slip, or loss of our sobriety. When this happens, we all seem to share similar emotions, and we can depend on other members of S-Anon to understand and to help us get back on the right track.

● ● ●

MEMBERS SHARE

Sobriety Is... Sobriety in S-Anon is about me and the way I treat myself and whether I can look at my mirrored image and love the person I see. Sobriety is knowing and owning all of my own behaviors and choices. Sobriety is knowing that I am a grateful, recovering member of S-Anon because I have a problem that I am choosing to do something about. It means that I will always need S-Anon no matter what may become of the sexaholics in my life.

Stop Playing God... For me, a slip is going back to the way I used to act and react before I came into the S-Anon Program. I used to believe that I had to control others and that I was responsible for their behavior. For example, I was sexual with my husband before he traveled, thinking that it would make him less likely to look at other women while he was away from home. In S-Anon I learned that for my own recovery and for the good of the people I love, I had to stop trying to control everything. I found that people need to learn and do things for themselves. Even if I believe I have all the answers, I need to let people figure it out in their own way. I still have to bite my tongue in order not to explain to my husband my opinions about why he's feeling the way he is, how it relates to his family of origin, and what he can do about it. Often I still want to control, manage, and be responsible, and I do have slips. After all, it took a long time to develop the habits I brought into the program, and I know today that nobody is perfect. In recovery I'm learning that although I may not have a choice about feeling these feelings, I have a choice about whether to act on them or not. With time it has gotten easier to recognize these feelings for what they are, without having to act on them.

Items on Several Members' Sobriety Lists… Being sober in S-Anon includes:

■ **Not wanting to be an object.** When I finally got sober in this program I decided to go through my closet and throw away or donate most of my clothes. Today I am comfortable with who I am and I don't need to dress suggestively to try and get attention from others.

■ **Staying in the moment.** Each day, each moment needs to be appreciated for what it is.

■ **Not regretting or resenting the past.** When I get overly focused on what I didn't do well or how someone hurt me or used me, I'm stuck somewhere other than today and am not really sober.

■ **Not getting stuck in fear of the future.** I am not sober when I am wondering what the future is going to be like and wanting to control it and wanting to make sure that I'm not going to get hurt.

■ **Minding my own business and working my own program.** Sobriety is not taking other people's inventories and deciding what they should or should not do in their lives. I can own the fact that I don't like the way someone is acting, but when I decide, for example, what meetings my husband should or should not go to, I'm not minding my own business. That kind of behavior reflects trying to play God for him.

- **Looking at myself and at life realistically.** Accepting people and situations in my life is a critical tool that helps me focus on S-Anon sobriety. Something that helps me to do that is the paragraph on Acceptance found in the AA Big Book p. 417 (*Alcoholics Anonymous*, Fourth Edition):

  "Acceptance is the answer to *all* my problems today. When I am disturbed, it is because I find some person, place, thing, or situation — some fact of my life — unacceptable to me, and I can find no serenity until I accept that person, place, thing, or situation as being exactly the way it is supposed to be at this moment. Nothing, absolutely nothing, happens in God's world by mistake. Until I could accept my alcoholism [powerlessness over sexaholism], I could not stay sober; unless I accept life completely on life's terms, I cannot be happy. I need to concentrate not so much on what needs to be changed in the world as on what needs to be changed in me and in my attitudes."

- **Keeping the focus on myself.** When I am sober in this program I take control of my own actions and change what I can about myself, not other people.

- **Being honest about who I am and how I feel.** Most of my acting out before I came to S-Anon was really acting *in*. I sometimes seemed more "sober" then because I was so out of touch with my emotions. Sometimes I still don't want to appear vulnerable and would like others to think I am "just fine," when I am most emphatically not "just fine." I am learning that it's not necessarily a slip or a bad thing to be angry, fearful, or whatever. It's okay for me to feel and acknowledge my emotions, and I didn't used to know that. To be sober, though, I need to dig a little deeper, beneath the disturbing emotions, examine the reasons why I am hurt or fearful, and become willing to surrender those attitudes or areas of my life to my Higher Power for healing. For me, this is the process of "staying sober."

- **Setting healthy boundaries with people.** My mother is the sex addict who affected my life the most, and I used to take care of her a lot and resented every minute of it. That wasn't good for me and it wasn't right for her, no matter what she did to me in my childhood. I didn't want to have the emotional hangovers I got when I would stay too long on the phone and end up screaming at her. For my own sobriety and peace of mind, I set a boundary around our visits and telephone calls, because spending too much time with her is not a sober situation for me.

Failure to Act... My husband said something to me one night that affected my self-image. I cried for half an hour. For the next day and a half every time he looked at me, I was moping and pouting. I could have asked for help, but I never turned to my Higher Power. I guess I preferred to wallow in self-pity. Looking back, I can see that in a situation like this, part of it (the hurt feelings and the crying) was beyond my control, and the other part of it (the wasted day and a half) happened because I did not take any action to correct my thinking. I didn't call anyone, I didn't take a walk or try to do anything for myself. For me, that was a loss of my sobriety—a slip.

Acting As If... I had been learning in S-Anon that I had been doing lots of things that were keeping me from serenity and peace of mind, and it seemed impossible that I would ever be able to stop doing all those things. Later on, I began to realize that I would have little chance of changing my behavior in any kind of lasting way if my attitude didn't change as well. My controlling, angry, self-righteous, self-willed, fearful, obsessive thinking was at the root of my problems. Yet how could I stop being angry, for example? I was also learning that I was entitled to my feelings, and that I had to acknowledge my real feelings, and not deny them and pretend to be something I wasn't. I realized that emotional sobriety might be many years away if I waited for my feelings and attitudes to change just because I wanted them to. I decided to ask my Higher Power to remove my shortcomings, and in the meantime to help me, in certain situations, to "act" sober, even if I wasn't feeling particularly sober at the time. It works, one day and one behavior at a time!

Recognizing Loss of Sobriety... I struggle with my sobriety often, and I can certainly define what it isn't. I know that I have lost it when I dig through my spouse's briefcase to read his journal. I know that I have lost it when I drive to where my spouse works to see if his car is in the parking lot when he does not answer my phone call. I know that I have lost it when I go through his dresser drawers looking for evidence. I know I have lost it when I look under my son's bed for pornography. I have done all these things and more. I know I have lost it because the behavior is pre-meditated and while I am doing these things my fear of being "caught" produces physical stress responses. I sweat, breathe rapidly, my heart rate increases, and I want to either fight with someone or run away. When I do lose it, I try to take corrective action. When I read the journal, I told my spouse, my therapist and my S-Anon group. Knowing that I will "own" my behavior afterward now helps me to keep from slipping again. I no longer have pre-disclosure blind faith in the relationship, but I believe that if I need to know something or find something out, God will reveal it, and I do not have to go looking for it.

RECOVERING IN OUR
RELATIONSHIPS

‿

Sexaholism has affected us deeply whether the sexaholic in our lives was a marriage partner, significant other, parent, sibling, or another family member. Perhaps the sexaholic was a good friend, teacher, or boss. It also seems true that whenever and however sexaholism has invaded our lives, it has caused our interactions with others to become more complicated and confused.

Often we have found it difficult to see how someone else's sexual attitudes and behavior could impact us so much. We may have wondered why we should need help when the other person has the problem with sexual lust. It may have been difficult for us to admit that sexual addiction is possible and that it is a progressive disease much like alcoholism. We may have come to S-Anon to find relief from the pain. As our awareness has grown, and as we have begun using the tools of the S-Anon Program, we have found strength and hope to move forward in our lives. We can choose recovery whether or not the sexaholic does.

We cannot know for sure that our relationship with the sexaholic will ever be what we might have wished for, but we do know that we can learn to trust a Higher Power and the process of recovery. We are assured that there is no unhappiness too great to be lessened. In S-Anon, we learn that we need to concentrate on our own recovery. We learn to keep the focus on ourselves and trust that a Higher Power will guide us through the challenges in our relationships.

Part Two

WHEN THE SEXAHOLIC IS A SPOUSE OR PARTNER

Although we are urged to focus on ourselves in recovery, we face the extra challenge of learning new ways of being together with our partner. Recovering in this type of relationship presents us with a variety of issues. How can we trust a person who has proven untrustworthy? How can we communicate honestly with each other when we haven't for so long? Can our sexual relationship ever be a joyful and fulfilling expression of our commitment to each another? We had thought we were committed, but how long should we wait for real change to occur? What if the sexaholic does not choose recovery?

Questions such as these can bring up fear, and our thinking may become confused and distorted. The experiences of S-Anon members with sexaholism in a spouse or partner are diverse. Personal safety, the risk of sexually transmitted diseases, and the safety of children are considerations we may face when determining how to handle our specific situations. In S-Anon, we do not give advice on these matters; we share from our own experiences.

In S-Anon we learn that the sexaholic is powerless over lust, and that we are powerless over the sexaholic and his or her behavior. We are also powerless over our own compulsions to try to control or fix our partner and our relationship. We may have thought we knew the reason for the sexaholic's problem and that we could help him or her. We may have tried many methods including pleading, crying, threatening, giving ultimatums, walking out, coming back, joining in on the acting out behavior, reasoning, monitoring, ignoring, or punishing. We learn that we did not cause the sexaholism, we cannot control it, and we cannot cure it. Sexaholism is a family disease, meaning that we, too, have become spiritually and emotionally ill, and we need help.

As we begin our recovery, we learn to let go of shame and guilt, and we become able to share with others--feeling accepted just as we are. We learn to trust in a Higher Power of our own understanding and make good choices. We see that serenity, dignity, and emotional growth are possible. In S-Anon we begin our own recovery by working the Twelve Steps and Twelve Traditions of S-Anon and applying the S-Anon principles to our lives. As we focus on our own recovery, one day at a time, and not on our partner's recovery, we will soon begin to see the benefits, including God's gift of serenity.

The following section includes some experience, strength, and hope from S-Anon members who are recovering from the effects of sexaholism in a spouse or partner.

• • •

MEMBERS SHARE ON TRUST

It Takes Time... People who know about our problems say to me, "How could you ever trust your husband again?" The short answer is "time." That is, over time he has given me reason to trust him again by acting in a trustworthy manner. So I've gotten to the point that even when unusual things happen, I no longer automatically jump to the conclusion that it is related to my husband's sexaholism. I trust my Higher Power to alert me to what I need to know. The basic intimacy is now there.

Trusting in a Higher Power First... I'm beginning to see that trusting my Higher Power underlies learning to trust in all areas of my life. I'm learning that turning it over to my Higher Power and surrendering my will, allows me to be open to finding the solution. This is particularly true when I'm struggling in my relationship with my partner. It has never failed that after surrendering, within a short period of time there seems to be something changing. I often don't know whether the change is in me or my partner or both of us, but changes happen, and then healing starts. Surrendering to my Higher Power is working for me. Turning my will and my life over to my Higher Power is the only tool I know that has saved me at times when I was at my lowest and didn't know where to turn next.

Trust is... Trust doesn't mean that my wife is always going to be there for me, that she is always going to agree with me, or that she is always going to meet my needs. That's unhealthy selfishness, not trust. As I am applying the S-Anon principles to my life, I have confidence that my Higher Power will be there for me and meet my needs. I need to also take care of myself and carefully listen to my own needs and desires. I am learning to trust myself in our relationship. I am learning to ask for what I need, not expect her to read my mind, and not try to control the outcome. My wellbeing is no longer dependent on her.

A Realistic Trust... As I grew in the S-Anon Program and began to seek my Higher Power, something began happening in me. I didn't force it — it simply came in God's time. I began to trust again. But now it's not a blind kind of trust. Today I know that human beings have diseases and that they fail, but God does not fail. As long as I continue to trust my Higher Power with my life, I believe that I will be OK.

• • •

MEMBERS SHARE ON COMMUNICATION AND HONESTY

Fear of Intimacy... I have been afraid to communicate with my spouse, especially regarding difficult subjects. I tend to avoid saying anything, or I tell little white lies because sometimes I feel afraid to tell the truth. But recently when my husband said he felt that I was distant sexually, I was able to work through the fear and admit that he was right. That was a lot of growth for me. It was so hard to admit my part, because I would rather live in denial and believe in the "magic fix," rather than have to say how I feel. I, too, am afraid of intimacy, but our communication has grown by leaps and bounds as a result of both of us working our programs. I'm learning how to get over the fears that have held me back.

The Importance of Listening... I feel that our communication improves if I surrender trying to figure out what the other person is thinking — what they "really want" and what they "really mean" — and simply listen. For example, I wanted to talk about a difficulty that my daughter was having in her relationship. My husband really didn't want to hear about it because it was painful for him. He was able to say this in a non-threatening way that was simply stating his feelings, and somehow I was able to hear him! My automatic reaction was to be critical of him, but I was able to stop myself from saying the things that would have turned our communication off. Instead, we talked about his feelings about hearing other people's troubles, particularly those of someone close to him, rather than focusing on our daughter. It was truly a wonderful moment of intimacy and true communication.

Honesty or Dumping?... I know I need to examine the motivation behind my "honesty." Sometimes my motivation to share is to "dump" or to get a specific reaction out of my partner. That is not honesty. That is manipulation and it always has an ulterior motive. So when I want to share something "honestly" with my partner, I need to be mindful of my motives. Honesty, along with the motivation of sharing who I am, does a lot to strengthen our relationship.

Sharing Who I Am... I see that being committed in a relationship doesn't mean giving up myself, it means being honest about who I am, and being courageous enough to share the reality of myself with someone else, regardless of what that person is going to say. It means not being a chameleon anymore.

Learning to Communicate... I used to be so afraid of conflict; if I didn't like something my husband had said or done, I would just withdraw and not talk to him about it. Sometimes I'd hardly say a word to him for days, until finally I'd get over feeling hurt or angry. Of course, nothing would really have changed. My husband said that he felt I was punishing him, but he didn't know why. After some time in recovery I got to be comfortable with writing him letters about whatever was bothering me. I was surprised and gratified at his willingness to consider my side of things. Now communication is clearer between us. If I'm upset or hurt about something, I ask him to listen without answering until I'm through telling him my feelings, even if this means my talking for 15 minutes or more. Then he gets a chance to respond without my interrupting. We continue this pattern until we both feel satisfied that we've been heard and understood. Talking this way about our feelings, rather than carrying resentments around for days, has greatly improved our relationship.

Gentle Honesty... I'm aware that I can sometimes observe others and sense what's going on with them. But I can also use that intuition as a weapon. Lately I've seen myself hurting my husband with my honesty. For example, when I perceived that my spouse was in a fog, I was sure to be "honest" with him, pointing out very clearly just what I thought he was doing or not doing. I know honesty is a tool of the program, but hopefully it is a gentle tool and not a tool with which I abuse my partner.

• • •

MEMBERS SHARE ON HEALTHY SEXUALITY

I Am Not Alone... Hearing honest sharing on healthy sexuality as well as other topics from S-Anon members reinforces for me that I am not alone; that there are other people who have worked through these same issues; and that in recovery, my relationship and my sex life can improve. It is such a relief to be able to share with others on personal issues, such as intimacy and sex. When I share about my fears and problems they seem to lose their power over me. I don't feel so overwhelmed. Knowing that other people are struggling and working through the same things I am gives me great hope.

Keeping the Focus on Myself... When I first heard the statement "sex was optional," I actually translated it to mean that *I* would become "optional" to my partner — a truly terrifying thought! At that time my sexuality was completely tied in with being passively desirable, available, and receptive. I had no concept of my own sexuality as separate from the demands or desires of my partner. I resented having to put the focus on myself and examine these ideas. The periods of abstinence that we agreed upon sometimes seemed too long, but I was actually relieved not to have to deal with sex in early recovery. I thought that the friendship and intimacy we had developed during our abstinence period leading up to our marriage would spill over into our sexual relationship, but they did not. My resentment at having to deal with the issue and my fear of physical intimacy were still present, and I secretly continued to blame my partner for what I now realize were my problems.

Finally I admitted to him that I had always been afraid of sex. I had purposely hidden my real feelings because I was afraid it meant that I was an inadequate woman at a very deep level. His loving, nonjudgmental acceptance of my feelings did much to alleviate the very fears that were causing the problem, and our sexual relationship has become much more fulfilling for me. I no longer feel that I am totally deficient in this area, and today I accept that in order for me to achieve "healthy" sexuality, I will have to continue to look at myself and share what I see with my partner. My husband and I are not going to experience healthy sexuality just because I love him. But working this program means that our sexual relationship can grow and change, too, just like the other areas of our marriage. For me, that is a miracle.

A Spiritual Union... I know that the improvement in the sexual part of our relationship is a gift of the program. What is helping me with healthy sexuality today is not focusing on the sex itself, but on the tools of the program that help me with all the other areas of my life, such as working the Steps, going to meetings, and trying to be honest with my spouse and other people. Doing these things week after week improves the spiritual part of my life whether I'm aware of it or not.

Most Important Sign of Love?... I've come to see that one stumbling block I kept tripping over was my basic belief that sex was supposed to bring fulfillment to our relationship, and that our sexual life together defined my sexual identity. It's difficult for sex to be "optional" if I'm basing my sexuality on how my partner is interacting with me sexually. In recovery I've had to start looking at myself, which has not been easy. I've realized that during sex I want to orchestrate the outcome and expect that it will make me feel whole and complete. So, I believe the best thing I can do for myself right now is not to put so much emphasis on sex, and keep on surrendering my desire to control it. I realize I have to let go of my unhealthy expectations and fantasies about sexuality.

Establishing Boundaries... In recovery I'm learning to participate sexually with my husband only when I feel I am emotionally
ready to be intimate. This means that I have had to learn to say "no"
on occasion, and sometimes have even stopped having sex if I began
to feel uncomfortable. I need to talk about my feelings with my husband and ask for what I need. It has become clear that non-sexual
touching is an important element in establishing that emotional intimacy for me. When emotional intimacy has been there as a foundation, sex has been wonderful. It has been true spiritual union.

Sex Is Optional?... During early recovery my husband said he
thought I was withholding sex as a punishment for what he'd done.
Sex triggered a lot of issues for me, because I knew that my husband
had been sexual with other people. Obsessive thoughts about his
acting out would pop into my head while we were in the middle of
sex, and it took quite a while for me to let go of them.

Today sex is optional, and I don't have to use it to find intimacy.
We're having sex less, both because it's optional and because there
are other changes in our life, like children. I'm more in tune with my
body and my needs, but I still struggle with the desire to take care
of him, wondering "If I'm the only person he can have sex with, am
I making it too hard for him?" and "If we go too long without having sex, will other people start to look more attractive to him?" I still
struggle with those old tapes, but I'm learning to keep focused on
myself and to have sex with my husband only when I feel comfortable. My recovery is a process and so is our communication about
sex.

ABSTINENCE

Some of us have found that abstaining from sex for a period of time allowed us to focus on ourselves while we dealt with the shock of discovery. Some of us have struggled with this suggestion, especially if it came from the sexaholic. We may have thought that a prolonged period of abstinence required a great deal of personal sacrifice, especially if we believed that the sexaholic had been withholding sex before recovery. It has been a lifesaving measure for those of us who felt at risk of sexually transmitted diseases. No matter how long we have been in recovery, a period of sexual abstinence can be a helpful way to gain insight into ourselves and our relationships by taking sex out of the equation.

As with all other personal matters, S-Anon takes no position on abstinence; we include below some sharing from members who have experience with periods of abstinence in their relationship.

When we are the ones requesting the period of abstinence, many of us have found it useful to first discuss our plans with our sponsor, and examine our motives. We have found that using abstinence in an attempt to manipulate or seek revenge on the sexaholic, rendered the experience futile, or even destructive. Many couples have agreed upon a period of time for the abstinence and a time to renegotiate or end the abstinence period. When discussing our desire for abstinence with our partner, it is suggested that we choose a calm time and speak in terms of our own needs and feelings.

• • •

MEMBERS SHARE ON ABSTINENCE

Discoveries... My spouse and I have had a number of abstinence agreements; some he initiated, others I did. For us the agreements meant no intercourse or sexual touching for a set period of time. I discovered different things with each period of abstinence. I learned that I could survive without sex. I became painfully aware that I had difficulty keeping and enforcing the sexual boundaries we had set together. I learned that I had been so focused on my spouse's sexual needs that I had become disconnected from my own body rhythms and desires. I became aware that I had difficulty being emotionally vulnerable with my spouse. I also learned that I had a lot of body shame. These insights have been incredibly helpful to my recovery.

Defining Intimacy... In our marriage, my husband was sexually aggressive with me. As his disease escalated, he became increasingly disinterested in me sexually. Sex was still his "drug," but I could no longer be his "fix." I thought that if I could just get him interested in having sex with me, we would live happily ever after. Instead, I continued to feel more rejected and inadequate as a woman. My husband did not choose recovery, but I began attending S-Anon. After five months in S-Anon, I realized that it was important that our sexual relationship complement the intimacy in the rest of our relationship. I became aware that there was no intimacy in the rest of our relationship. This awareness gave me the courage to stop trying to get my husband to be sexual with me. I needed a period of abstinence so I could begin to focus on myself. I also wondered if my husband and I could be friends or experience other ways of being intimate with each other outside of having sex.

Sex Is Optional... I felt resentful when my spouse told me that we would need to go through a period of abstinence. It wasn't so much that I missed having sex with him, I just resented being told what to do by a person who had hurt me deeply in this area. The first gift of the abstinence, however, was an awareness that my partner was serious about his recovery. I learned to respect his desire for abstinence, rather than seeing it as a challenge to my powers of persuasion. I also needed to look at our relationship without the false intimacy I had found in the past by being sexual. I would never have even begun to find out the truth about myself if we had continued to be sexual in the old way. Other gifts have been a better understanding of my sexuality and an in-depth acceptance of the mystery and difficulty of a sexual relationship. I have a high level of comfort with the idea that "sex is optional." This statement made no sense to me as long as I thought that sex was the most important sign of love.

Abstinence and Being Single... When I became single in S-Anon, I was scared to death of the dating process. I wasn't ready to have a new relationship because I hadn't yet sorted out my issues around my own sexuality. As I progressed in recovery, my attitudes gradually changed. I learned that I didn't have to be sexual with others, but found I could hold onto my sexuality and cherish it as a beautiful part of me. When I no longer equated sex with love and intimacy and had true comfort with my own sexuality, then I could think about dating. I loved myself enough and had enough recovery to be able to express my sexual wants and needs, and accepted that it was okay not to be sexually intimate with someone. The level of honesty with which I now relate to others could not have come about without the growth I experienced during a period of abstinence.

Facing my Fear... Like many others, I believed that sex was the most important sign of love. I looked for reassurance through sex; when my husband found me sexually attractive, then I felt like a worthwhile person. I thought that if it weren't for sex he would probably leave me. A period of abstinence brought me face to face with these beliefs. I recognized for the first time how much of my self-esteem came from believing I was sexually attractive. It was good for me to face my fear that my spouse wanted me only for my body, because it was the first step toward changing those old beliefs. I began to see that I, too, used sex as a short-cut to, or a substitute for, intimacy. I had never learned how to touch or hug or kiss without it leading to sex, so a period of abstinence was a good opportunity for me to learn new ways to be intimate.

Taking Care of Myself... When my husband and I were new in recovery, I honestly didn't care if I ever had sex with him again. I was so shocked to find out about his behavior, and so confused about my feelings about him and about the future of our relationship, I could hardly bear to sleep in the same bed with him—so I chose not to do so. It was something I needed in order to deal with the stress in my life at that time.

Most Important Sign of Love?... Not having sex with my husband? It was a revolutionary idea! Our marriage was, so I thought, based on sex. What was going to happen if we did not have sex? Part of the sexual addiction in our home showed itself in our relationship. I was used to having sex on a daily basis, if not more often. My feelings of being loved were largely based on the fact that my husband very frequently wanted to have sex with me. In order to avoid arguments, I had long ago given up trying to say "No" when I did not want sex, and I had felt that I could count on a fairly smooth relationship by giving in. Then my husband began attending recovery meetings for his sexaholism. And I started attending S-Anon meetings.

After we had attended our respective groups for several months, he asked if we could go through a period when we did not have sex. Being angry and resentful, I replied that I had had enough sex for a lifetime and that abstinence was fine with me.

But was it really "fine?" What happened to me during that period of not having sex was incredible. I became very fearful that my marriage would not last, that my husband would leave, that I was not attractive to him, and that we would disagree even more. I began to realize that I used sex in an unhealthy way, too! For example, I would start an argument and see how long it would take me to manipulate my husband into bed, thereby dissolving our argument. I flaunted myself in front of him to satisfy my need to know that, indeed, he did "love" me because we would then go to bed. The tool I had used so successfully to manipulate my husband had been taken from me. But I learned that I could live in the same house, share the same bed, touch, hug and kiss my husband without having to have intercourse. I learned that I needed to communicate using words, rather than manipulation. I learned that even without sex I could still have a marriage and an even better relationship with my husband.

When my husband wanted to end the period of abstinence, I had grown enough to say "No," and we had a period of 21 months in our marriage when we did not have intercourse. Would we ever have sex again? It was very frightening for me to realize that the decision of when I was again ready to be sexual would be mine to make. I ended the period of abstinence with the knowledge that I was loved for myself, not just for my body, and that I had become a woman who could love and participate more fully in a sexual union. Abstinence was a crucial part of my growth in S-Anon, even though I was not the one to initiate it. I am very grateful that I did have the opportunity to learn that sex can be an extension of an inti-mate relationship and not the only basis for our marriage. Today I feel cared for in our marriage, and I can give as well as receive.

• • •

MEMBERS SHARE ON COMMITMENT

Giving the Program Time to Work... When I first started com-ing to meetings, I just wanted to leave the marriage and all the prob-lems behind. But I heard a lot of people talking about giving the program some time, so I decided that I would do just that: I would give it six months and see what happened. When six months passed I thought, "I'm not ready to leave, but I'm not sure I want to stay either." By that time my spouse and I were attending a lot of recov-ery meetings and working our respective programs. I decided to give it another six months, and that's the way I got through my first year. After a year I was able to start looking at it "one day at a time." For me it was important to address my attitudes and behavior with the help of S-Anon while in the relationship and not to simply run.

Commitment to Myself and My Higher Power... I'm a lot more committed to myself today, because I'm learning who I am and what I need. Although I've always been committed to my Higher Power, that commitment is changing, too. It is not just a commit-ment to a way of life in which I was brought up. It is a real commit-ment, born out of my desperation and out of need. Now my commitment to marriage means I can love my partner best by totally letting go of trying to control the relationship. This is hard to explain, but I'm recognizing he's an individual person, and I'm an individual person. He has choices to make; I've got choices to make. If he chooses to live in his addiction, I can choose to stay in my recovery. I've felt a lot of deep confusion and hurt. In recovery I'm learning to love and respect myself and my partner, and I'm com-mitted to showing that by letting go.

Commitment to Reality... I can see now that before recovery I was committed to fantasies of what I wanted things to be like, particularly in my relationship with my husband. Today when I have difficulty in our relationship, it is often due to my bumping up against my old ideas of how things "should" be. In recovery I'm learning that commitment means being committed to the dynamic process of life the way it is, and that I can't control the other person or the outcome. Committing myself to hanging in there—when pain, loss, and conflict are inevitable—is really hard for me. Through working the program, I'm beginning to accept the inevitability of pain and change. Today my commitment means that I am committed to my recovery with the reality, not the fantasy, of who my husband is, as well as who I am and who I'm becoming. It also means that I must surrender my self-righteous attitude that I have all the answers and that I know the way everything should be.

Fear of Abandonment... It's much easier to be committed to my S-Anon recovery, my sponsor, or to my work than it is to be committed to my wife. I'm plagued by the old fear of "If I commit to her and she leaves, then I'll be devastated." In recovery I know that with my Higher Power's help her choice to leave will not devastate me. By keeping the focus on myself those old fearful feelings lose their grip on me. Part of my recovery is learning how to be vulnerable, honest, and committed while keeping the focus on myself.

Letting Go of Control... When I decided that I couldn't fix our marriage and that I could only participate in it, it finally began to be a real marriage for me. When I finally stopped viewing it as a term paper or a class where if I only did all my homework it would work, I started to understand and live the principles of the program. I've found that in recovery, only when I do the healthy things I have been reluctant to do, and let go of the unhealthy things that I have grasped so tightly, do I find the things that I've been looking for all along.

No Guarantees... Nothing in life is guaranteed. Despite actively working his recovery program, weekly counseling sessions, and a long period of sobriety, my husband recently had a relapse. This was very painful and frightening for me. Even though I was hurting, I was immediately able to utilize the tools of my S-Anon Program. I shared with him how I felt. I asked for help from my Higher Power. I called my sponsor. I dragged myself to church, and made a decision to renew my commitment to my own recovery. This included: asking trusted friends for prayer and accepting their offers of babysitting; calling friends in the program and checking in with them again and again; attending my S-Anon meeting and sharing my story; writing in my journal each night no matter how tired I was; calling my therapist for an emergency appointment; and writing this share. It helped me to review Step One: I am powerless over his compulsions to act out sexually; Step Two: God can restore my sanity; and Step Three: my plans and life are safe in my Higher Power's hands. I know that nothing happens by coincidence. God had a reason for my finding out about my husband's relapse. Although I am shaken up, I am still grateful for God's wisdom and plan.

Living with an Active Sexaholic... I have asked myself so many questions: What does it mean that I am still living with an active sex addict? Have I just not recovered enough to separate? What are the underlying effects on our children? What are my "bottom lines?" When I finish asking myself the questions that have yet to be answered, I come back to the reality of the First Step: I am powerless over sexaholism, and my life becomes unmanageable when I try to manage the lives of others. What about self-deception? Am I crazy to be living with an active sexaholic, given the progressive nature of his disease? Today I believe that no plan of my own could have given me the willingness to change and mend my ways. I know more will be revealed to me as I continue to rely on my Higher Power and work the S-Anon Program. The peace I have today is a gift from my Higher Power. I am so sure of God's love that I can leave my concerns in His hands, knowing that I and those I love will be provided for "one day at a time." I believe that God will not leave me without a way out, even when I mistakenly interpret His will or my place in a situation. As long as I am willing to accept where I am, honestly, and be open to His help, it is easy to make the next decision to trust God and turn my life over to His care.

WHEN THE SEXAHOLIC IS NOT A SPOUSE
OR PARTNER

Help can be found in S-Anon no matter what type of relationship we have or have had with a sexaholic. Some of us were affected by active sexaholism at an early age– either sexually abused or otherwise exposed to an inappropriate sexual environment. The sexual attitudes and behavior in our family of origin may have made us feel uncomfortable, and we may not have understood why we felt the way we did. Sometimes it wasn't until we had made some progress in our S-Anon recovery that we started to recognize how we were affected by someone else's problem with lust. Sexaholism is a family disease and it affects all family members in some way.

Some of us have seen our children manifesting symptoms of sexaholism or choosing sexaholics as their friends and partners. Watching them hurt themselves, their families, jobs, and futures is distressing. We may have tried to help them or control them, or we may have believed them and their promises to change. Our fear and guilt have brought us to the point of despair. S-Anon offers us tools to heal in these relationships, too. We can find serenity for ourselves by working the tools of the S-Anon Program.

Some of us were affected by the sexaholism of someone outside the family; perhaps a teacher, medical professional, clergy member, a person who holds a position of authority, or someone perceived to be in authority. In S-Anon we learn that we cannot cause, control, or cure anyone's sexual compulsions. The behavior of the sexaholic is not our responsibility. S-Anon offers help and hope to all whose lives have been or are being affected by the disease of sexaholism; there is a solution. The following section includes the experience, strength, and hope of S-Anon members recovering from the effects of sexaholism in someone other than a spouse or partner.

•   •   •

MEMBERS SHARE—SEXAHOLIC FAMILY MEMBERS

Adult Child of a Sexaholic... My father's sexaholism had a profound impact on me. I lived under a cloud of impending disaster, even when things were going fine. I couldn't see the harmful effects on my life of living with and reacting to that dread. I had become too emotionally connected with my father—I didn't know where he left off and I began. Sexaholism was the big, bad secret in our family, and I loyally guarded that secret for years. In my family it was more important to give an appearance of being happy than to experience the genuine emotion. My main method of coping with the turmoil was to become over-involved with educational pursuits, with extra-curricular projects, and excessive religious activity.

When I left home and got married, I still relied on emotionally withdrawing and piling on activities when circumstances became difficult. I could justify everything I was doing, but I couldn't prevent my partner from feeling abandoned and unloved. She also reacted strongly toward my father's sexual acting out and refused to allow him to baby-sit for his grandchildren. When I felt forced to choose between my wife and my father, I clearly felt my life had become unmanageable, and I decided to get help.

Taking my First Step was painful, but as that Truth deep down inside of me came to the surface, I felt reunited with a deep part of myself, and it felt good. My pain had begun when the effects of my father's sexaholism began to affect me emotionally and spiritually. It was only when life became hopeless that I surrendered, took my First Step, and gave God a chance to restore my life.

Overcoming Bitterness... I grew up in a sexaholic household. My grandfather sexually abused me from age two to age six. My older brothers began to sexually abuse me when I was seven until I was fourteen. Then my father sexually abused me for a year, until I was fifteen. I thought that if I loved someone, I had to give them whatever they wanted. To me, sex was definitely the most important sign of love. I always seemed to be attracted to the same type of person, and I was always confused.

I went on to date sexaholics and to marry a sexaholic. That relationship became violent; at one point we started to physically fight, and the person who broke it up said "I think if that fight had   75 gone on, you would have killed him." I believe that is true. My life was a cycle of pain, and I was even fired from a job due to my obsession with a sexaholic.

I began recovery in another Twelve-Step program. Aware of my issues with my family of origin, I sensed that there was more work to be done, but I didn't know exactly what work it was and I feared the pain of exploring these issues. Ten years later, God led me to S-Anon. My first S-Anon meetings were at an S-Anon International Convention, and it was there that I saw my first glimmer of hope. The closing speaker introduced himself as a sexaholic when he got up to share. I looked at him and thought to myself, "I don't have to hate them anymore. I don't have to resent them. I don't have to want revenge, and I don't have to live in the bitterness." That was the beginning of hope for me.

I have experienced so much healing in S-Anon. Yes, I grew up in a sexaholic family, but today I have the freedom of no longer expecting more from them than they can give. They are suffering from the disease of sexaholism.

S-Ateen Story... I knew about the sexaholism in our family. My parents were in the process of a divorce, when one night I received a phone call from my father, who said that he needed to tell me that he had sexually abused me as a child and that the abuse would be reported to our local children's welfare agency. I know that if I had not been in S-Ateen and not had a program and a sponsor, I probably would not be here today. My sponsor let me cry it all out and helped me accept my feelings. I began to understand that even though this was very painful and sad, that everything was going to be all right; that God had a reason even for this.

The children's welfare agency did press charges against my father on my behalf, and my father served a year in jail. I love my father so much, and I felt guilty because I agreed to continue with the trial and felt partially responsible for his having to go to jail. I believed I had to do what I could to protect others whom he could possibly harm because of his profession. My S-Ateen sponsor and the people in my group told me it was not my fault; what had happened to me was because of my father's illness and the choices he made, and I was doing what I needed to do for my recovery.

S-Ateen has also been a great help in dealing with some difficult feelings about my mother. Part of my recovery has been to accept that my mother tried to do what was best in the situation, but also to accept that I still felt a lot of anger and resentment that she could not see what was going on. Sharing with other S-Ateens helped me work through that anger and resentment, and it helped me to realize that both of my parents were sick people, not bad people. They didn't mean to harm me. I know that eventually I will need to address my part in keeping the family secrets and the reasons why I did not come forward to talk to my mom about what was happening to me.

While working on Step Two, I realized that I also blamed God for allowing this situation to occur in the first place. I believed I had done nothing to deserve this abuse, and I asked myself why God would let this happen to me. I have come to believe that the God of my understanding does not have control over our decisions. He tries to show us the right way to go, but he does not make the decisions for us. And I realized that my Higher Power really is loving and caring. After all, He provided all the wonderful people in S-Anon and S-Ateen who have shared their experience, strength, hope, support, and courage with me.

Daughter of a Sexaholic Mother... My mother is the sexaholic who affected my life the most. She had affairs when my brother and sister were growing up; my brother was nineteen years old when I was born and my sister was almost thirteen. When I was six weeks old, my mother started leaving me with my aunt for the day, so she could be free to pick up men while my father was at work. When I was six months old, my family moved to the house where I grew up, and my mother was no longer able to walk to a bar or to a street corner to pick up men. Even though my mother stopped having affairs during my growing up years, she continued to be very flirtatious with men. I remember feeling ashamed of my mother. I would rarely invite friends to my home, and I was very aware that most of the other mothers in the neighborhood did not like my mother. Other family members also have confirmed my suspicions that my mother had an incestuous relationship with my brother. He also sexually abused me when I was a very young child.

I remember feeling so angry with God when I was a senior in high school and my father died, because I had my dad on a pedestal. I grew up thinking I had one terrible parent—my mother—and one wonderful parent—my father. Taking my father off the pedestal was an important piece of healing work in my early S-Anon recovery. I learned and accepted that my father was just as sick as my mother. My father did not protect me from abuse, and he did not make any attempts to get help for himself or his children.

My mother is now past eighty years old and she lives in a senior citizens' residence. She is still very flirtatious with men, and she has very few women friends because of her behavior. I do spend some time assisting her with chores and health care needs, but I still need to set firm boundaries when I'm with her. Today I can spend time with her without resentments and usually without losing my serenity. This is truly a gift that has come to me through working the S-Anon Program.

Sexaholic Caretaker... I was orphaned at 14 and went to live with my sister and her family. Her husband was the first sexaholic in my life. I was very needy, fragile, and impressionable. I soaked up any attention I could get and learned attitudes in this unhealthy environment that stayed with me as I grew up. What I believed in my teenage years was that women were responsible for meeting all of men's needs. I also learned that men's most important need was for sex. I thought my needs were not important, because I was told I was selfish if I voiced them. If I could not meet the needs of others, I thought I was a "failure" and "unlovable."

These unhealthy beliefs caused me to seek out equally unhealthy, often sexaholic, partners when I began dating. At age 18, my unhealthy world view led me to place myself in a situation in which I was raped. I was unable to report the crime or ask for help in dealing with its effects. In my thinking, it was my fault that it happened and my needs were inconsequential. My life was overshadowed by fear and loneliness, and I felt worthless. When I came to S-Anon I was shown how to begin to rebuild my life on a healthy and solid foundation. I learned that I am responsible only for my own needs and actions. I learned that I am powerless over all the other people in my life, their actions, decisions, and consequences. Finally, I learned that although I was definitely a participant in unhealthy relationships, the shortcomings of others are neither my fault nor my responsibility. It has been painful at times, but I have learned how to find serenity, healing, and love in my life. Today, because of S-Anon, I know a freedom and joy in living that I would have never thought possible.

Sexaholic Father... I was overwhelmed, confused, depressed and angry when I discovered that my father was a sexaholic. At first I was in shock and had no idea how to deal with the issue. I was so angry and thought that he was acting this way to hurt me. At first I kept myself busy with work and I chose not to deal with the issue, but soon I became even more depressed and began to isolate myself from friends. I was unsure who to turn to or where I should look for support. I knew I could no longer continue down my current path, so I started attending S-Anon meetings. After sharing my story, I felt as if a huge burden had been lifted from my shoulders. I shared the secret I had been keeping inside of me for years with people who understood and had been through similar circumstances. Through working the Steps and relying on the tools of the program and my Higher Power, I see a difference in myself and my attitude toward my father. Instead of being angry at him, I feel compassion for him; he is sick and does not realize it. S-Anon has been the greatest gift that I could have given myself. I know that I still have a long and difficult road of recovery ahead, but as long as I keep working the program and using the tools, my story will become one that carries a message of hope for new members.

Sibling Relationship... I was affected by the sexual behavior of family members. For instance, I became focused on my sister's needs and her many relationships. I lost touch with my own needs. I felt less important than any of her romantic relationships and became resentful. Although I came into S-Anon because of my husband's sexaholism, I was given the opportunity to grow and heal in this part of my life, too. I had blamed my sister for my low self-esteem and inability to have healthy relationships. Through working the S-Anon Program I have taken responsibility for my part in losing myself in her. I am grateful for the healing I see in myself and in my relationship with my sister.

• • •

MEMBERS SHARE—SEXAHOLISM IN A SON OR DAUGHTER

My Daughter's Sexaholism... My daughter was the second sex addict who deeply affected my life. Her sexaholism drew her into a relationship with a person who was on probation and had a criminal record. She would listen to no one; she had all the answers. At one point she came home to live, but I was no longer willing to enable a sex addict. I was becoming a healthier person; she was becoming less and less healthy. We very much wanted that mother-daughter relationship. We would cry about it, and we would talk about it, but it just wasn't possible. I confronted her with my suspicions and concerns and told her that she would have to move out out if she didn't stop acting out. She went back to her husband, but what followed was a fast downward spiral that ended disastrously for her. Although it is still painful to reflect upon, I believe I am at peace now with the fact that we were not able to connect during the times when the disease of sexaholism was active.

Detaching with Love... I entered S-Anon more than seven years ago, determined to save my 17 year marriage to a charismatic, deeply troubled sexaholic. Fourteen months later the sexaholic was gone, and my motivation for staying in S-Anon and working the program had changed. Now I was determined to pursue health for myself and my pre-teen and teenage children. I had learned that sexaholism is a family disease, and I was willing to do anything to stop its spread throughout our family. The first few years were difficult, especially for my sensitive 13-year-old son. All three of us were in therapy, attending spiritual support groups. When my son was 15, he began to attend an S-Ateen group, which helped him to deal with his unhappiness.

The year my son was 17 he gradually stopped attending S-Ateen meetings, stating that he had resolved many of his issues with his father and was getting all the support he needed from his spiritual and church youth groups. Shortly after his 18th birthday I was trying to locate my tax records on the computer and found, openly stored in the documents bin, a collection of pornography which clearly belonged to my son. My immediate desire was to react — find him at the school function he was attending, give free reign to my fear, and issue ultimatums. Thank God for six plus years in the program, and the knowledge of how counterproductive that would be. Instead, for support I called two S-Anon friends with older male children. Then I called one of my friends who is a recovering sexaholic and asked for his suggestions. Instead of obsessing, I went to bed and actually slept. In the morning I went to church and asked God to give me the right words. Fully 24 hours after finding the pornography I sat down to talk to my son about it. I did not ask him for any explanations or promises. Instead I told him how much I loved him. I also shared with him that, having watched this disease destroy his father, I was terrified of what it could do to him. I offered him resources, including the names and phone numbers of two men who were recovering sexaholics, who would be willing to meet with him one-on-one and take him to recovery meetings. Then I limited my input to daily heart-felt prayer for my son.

Fifteen months later God has not shown me any more pornography or signs that my son is sinking deeper into sexual addiction. Today I have the faith that my Higher Power will bring to my attention anything I need to know. I do not have to search, snoop, or question my son. Today I also know that, as much as I love him, this is my son's problem, not mine. He has the tools to deal with the disease—tools such as the knowledge of the effects and progressive nature of sexaholism, the opportunity through marathons (local or regional one-day conventions) and open speaker meetings to meet and listen to the stories of recovering sexaholics, and the experience of working an S-Ateen program. My son knows where to find help. The best way I can help him is to pray for him, be open for conversations, and leave him in God's hands. My perspective and attitude depend on my working my own program.

(For information about S-Ateen meetings see the *S-Anon/S-Ateen Service Manual* or contact the S-Anon World Service Office.)

Establishing Boundaries... I have learned a lot over the years about how to deal with my son's sexaholism. I learned early on that some of his behaviors were triggers for my own early abuse issues. The behaviors which impacted me had to do with suggestive clothing, pictures hanging in his room which he invited me to view, and bringing into my house the very provocative young woman he had just picked up at the grocery store. It felt very strange to admit that my own child could trigger my fears and misgivings. I found it best to just sit down with him and explain that I could not be around such behaviors as they tended to re-traumatize me. Those conversations were all about me and what I needed, not about him and what he was supposed to be doing with his life. I was in early recovery and had learned I had the right to set boundaries for myself, even with my children.

Setting boundaries seemed to help us both. My son found his own recovery program for his sexaholism about a year later. As a late teen, it was hard for him to fit in, but he kept going to meetings and began to find his way. At one point, he was picked up by an older woman, herself new in the program, and when I questioned the relationship he insisted they were "just friends." After a few weeks, it was obvious it was more than a friendship, and I was able to tell him he would have to move out of our home if he chose to continue the relationship. This was a difficult line to draw, for me, as I feared he would just move in with her, but I knew I had to let go of the outcome and just do my footwork. As it turned out, they stopped seeing each other soon after that.

Although he has often credited his sexaholism recovery program with saving his life, some years later, he decided it was too complicated to be a young, single person following the principles of that fellowship's program. Another gift of my program was learning that my children have their own Higher Power and I am not it! What a relief to realize that they rest in the care of a Power greater than their mother, regardless of the decisions they make.

Today, many years later, my son has chosen to work another Twelve Step program. My responsibility is to continue working the S-Anon Program and to turn over my concerns to my Higher Power. I never hide what I am doing if I am going to a meeting, but do not make it a big deal. He often takes me to the airport when I am head-ing for a program convention and asks how it was when I return. Today, relating to a 30-year-old man who is not my spouse, it seems that his personal life is none of my business unless it infringes upon mine in some way. He has been remarkably respectful of my needs. When I sense that he may be having difficulty, I just take my concern to my Higher Power and turn it over. I know that he is quite familiar with the tools and will find his way in God's time.

• • •

MEMBERS SHARE—SEXAHOLISM IN A PERSON
OUTSIDE THE FAMILY

Feeling Responsible... In high school I had a crush on my math teacher. I noticed that when the students were working at their desks he would pace around at the front of the class, and I could see that he was looking at girls' legs. I hated this about him, and I tried to dismiss it as if I were imagining it. I was always very careful about how I sat if I had on a skirt. So, already I was practicing "denial" and feeling responsible for someone else's behavior.

Seeing My Part... In college I was shy and had not yet had any boyfriends. I took an interactive course that was also a trip, and got close to one of the leaders. I knew he was married and had a baby, but somehow I thought that whatever he did was okay. We talked together and were sometimes alone together talking about personal subjects. Eventually he kissed and hugged me. I loved the attention and believed that he must be in control of himself and be able to share this kind of love with me. When the course was over, I just saw less and less of him. I did get involved with other men after that, but months later, I heard news about this professor. Apparently he was asked to resign from the college for inappropriate sexual conduct. It wasn't until then that I realized his behavior with me was also inappropriate. I felt used and taken advantage of by someone I had learned was dishonest. Years later, as I work on issues in S-Anon because of my partner's sexaholism, I have begun to see the dishonesty of my own denial and am working to heal from the effects of this old relationship.

Trusting in God... I was affected by the sexaholism of a leader in my faith community. He did not directly mistreat me, but sexually abused my husband when my husband was a young adult. I did not know about this until several years into our marriage. My husband disclosed his sexaholism to me and soon after shared with me about his relationship with this man. As the shock sunk in, I felt betrayed not only by someone I trusted, but also by an institution that I had trusted. The faith community had been, I thought, a representative of the God I trusted. I withdrew and kept a cautious distance from many of the people there. When I went into churches I felt myself looking around and mentally picking out the sexaholics. Thankfully, through all of these intense feelings, I cried out to God. Using the Twelve Steps of S-Anon, my understanding of God grew. I believed that God stayed with me and did not abandon me in my pain. I am grateful for the healing and growth I have experienced through working the S-Anon Program. I learned that I could trust God. By trusting in the God of my understanding and using the principles of the S-Anon Program, I chose again to participate in my faith community, knowing that we are all human. I believe I can be one among others in this community now and have come to embrace the truth in the slogan "There, but for the Grace of God, go I."

Watching the Watchers... I must admit I have obsessed and wasted time observing complete strangers who seem "drunk" from their sexual obsessions. I can catch wandering eyes and heads turning to take a quick or long "drink." I've seen it happen in the subway and even from my car. It was God's grace that led me to understand that my behavior of looking down on these people and judging them as active addicts is no better than the behavior of the people I have watched. I can get just as "drunk" and out of touch with reality as any active "addict." When I catch myself starting to put the focus on others, I pray and ask God to fill my mind with one of his ideas. God has brought me many beautiful ideas on which to focus.

Commitment to Recovery... Some women from the sexaholics' recovery meeting that met at the same time as my S-Anon meeting asked my S-Anon group if they could use our room to hold a women's sexaholic recovery meeting for the hour prior to our meeting. I was furious. *How dare they encroach on our turf? What if we wanted to meet earlier, and they would be in our way? This is "our" room; let them go find a room for themselves.* I wasn't alone in this thinking; the fear and reactions were contagious.

In the meantime, as Higher Power would have it, they contacted the church and were provided another room. As I look back, I can see how inhospitable I had been, and how I had gathered support for my fear from the other members. What was I afraid of? I was afraid that I wouldn't be able to take care of myself. I had forgotten that I had a Higher Power. I was still trying to assign blame and punishment for my pain. I had lost the ability to have compassion and was taking things way too personally. It didn't occur to me that these women were trying to get well, that they were saving their lives, just I was. I didn't feel safe and rather than work through it, I had reacted. I have discovered that I don't have to be afraid, and I am richer for it.

Part Two

HEALING IN ALL OUR RELATIONSHIPS

Often there is a lot of secrecy in families that are affected by sexaholism. In recovery, through working the tools of the program, we learn to be more honest and open with one another and to develop healthy communication. Even so, telling our children about our S-Anon Program is not easy, and we can benefit from taking time to pray, meditate, and consider how and when to approach it. The children may be supportive, but they may also react with anger and rejection. We can model healthy behavior with our children by practicing the program principles at home.

Many of us also had troubled relationships with extended family members and friends before we came to S-Anon. We may have felt the shame of having to cope with an addiction that affected the most personal and private area of our lives. We may not have been able to share our feelings and our problems with anyone—family, friends, or even therapists. We may have felt cut off from "normal" people and most of us at least partially have blamed ourselves. Sharing with others in S-Anon meetings opens the door to a new set of relationships with understanding people, but after a time many of us may want to share about ourselves and our recovery in a different way with other important people in our lives. We do not give advice on such matters, but we share from our own experiences. The following section is devoted to S-Anon members sharing how they dealt with their specific situations.

• • •

MEMBERS SHARE—RELATIONSHIPS WITH OUR CHILDREN

Opening My Eyes... My husband was incestuous with one of my daughters, and I knew nothing about it. He was living in his fantasy world, and I was living in my own. As I got into S-Anon recovery and my eyes began to open, I could see that there had been signs of the incest, but I never questioned my daughter. I had never talked to her about it. I am very aware that I was not the parent that she needed, and I am also aware that I did not have the tools at that time. Through working the S-Anon Program and applying the tools offered to me, I am making amends to my daughter. We have a growing relationship today and can share about our recovery. What a blessing!

No More Secrets… My four boys grew up in an unmanageable household due to the disease of sexual addiction in our home. We were the "looking-good family" on the outside and were shambles on the inside. They had experiences of having strangers brought into the home, a mother who was so focused on the sexaholic husband and his problems there was no time for them, and a father who who was acting out sexually.

Recovery from the disease of sexaholism and its effects came into our lives approximately 17 years ago. Our sons had been battered by unacceptable behavior on both of our parts and really did not know how to react to this new recovery behavior. They were told where we were going when we went to recover meetings or conventions, and there were no secrets about recovery. Literature from Twelve Step recovery programs was available so they could read it if they chose. They chose not to know anything about it, nor did they want to hear about it. As they grew and as we grew, our sons married and daughters-in-law came into our family. My husband told them that they were free to ask anything about his sexual addiction and he would answer them honestly. I told them I would take them to S-Anon if they so wished. Again, they did not want to know about our family history.

For us, the recovery process involved a steady growth; it was not an overnight event. Today, we are at ease with all of our children. Three of our sons and two of our daughters-in-law are in various recovery programs. Our family has evolved to the extent that our sons and daughters-in-law refer their friends who are struggling with sexual addiction problems to us for help. They know we are both active in our recovery programs and if they need help, we can direct them. We are now watching our grandchildren grow and wonder how the effects of recovery will trickle down to them. We have a true family now and thank our programs for leading us down the paths of recovery.

How Much to Reveal?... When I found out about my husband's addiction, our son had just had his eighth birthday. It was important at that point to tell him something about what was happening in our lives, because he was with me when I met my husband at the police station after a late night addiction-related arrest. The next morning my husband explained to our son that he had been arrested because he was somewhere that he should not have been. Our son accepted that. We told him if he wanted to talk to a counselor at school about it he could, but he should not tell his friends about it.

Once we began attending meetings, our son was quite curious about where we were going. We decided to tell him that we were going to meetings where we would learn about ourselves, which would help us have a better relationship and be better parents. At first, he said that he didn't think we needed to be better parents, but soon this explanation seemed to satisfy him. During the first six months of recovery, he would complain every time one of us went to a meeting. Eventually, he began to notice some changes in the way we were dealing with life and we were able to relate it back to what we had learned at the meetings.

My husband and I refer to the program in our son's presence without mentioning the specific name of the program or the addiction. We talk with him about what we have learned about ourselves and about recovery. He sees the tangible effects on our family life of the spiritual progress we have made as individuals.

My husband is infected with HIV as a result of acting out. This has a real impact on our discussions about what to tell our son about the addiction, and when to tell him. At this point, I believe we have given our son an appropriate amount of information. I also believe that God will help us to know what to disclose to him and how to do it in a loving way. The community of support we are building for ourselves is there for him when he is ready.

Achieving Balance... When I began my recovery, my children were all in elementary school. Our home had an atmosphere of tension and insecurity. I was bound and determined to be the perfect mother—loving, compassionate, understanding—but I really did not know how to manifest those qualities in a balanced way. I sometimes went to extremes in caring for my children. There was a constant feeling of impending disaster and if someone made a mistake (and there were plenty!), I reacted in extreme ways. I neglected the children emotionally, obsessing about my husband when he was acting out and worrying about the "next time" when he was not. I lived my life through my kids because I didn't even realize at that time that I had my own separate life. If they passed a science test, I felt I was a success. If they got a low grade, I was a failure as a mom. Their grades were my grades and their emotions became my emotions.

Today, after several years in S-Anon, my children know that when I go to a meeting, make a telephone call, or receive a telephone call from a program friend, I am trying to stay balanced. I don't force heavy conversation with my children, but I try to be aware of any opportunity where I might be able to share my recovery with them, and be emotionally available in that moment. I have told them that there are certain groups and people whom God has given to both their dad and me to help us learn how to truly love ourselves and others. I talk with them about being aware of feelings and learning to express feelings honestly in appropriate ways. I talk with them about the need for each of us to have boundaries, how we need to learn to "mind our own business" in a loving manner, and how I am not going to get this all perfect for probably a very long time — if ever! Above all, I try to make amends where needed as quickly as possible, and stay current with any issue needing our attention. I have not disclosed the details of their Dad's addiction. I feel that is his responsibility when he feels the time is appropriate.

Now, if I get off track, usually one of the children will bring it to my attention, and I again have the opportunity to put the program into practice! I cannot count the number of times my 13-year-old has said to me in so many words "Mom, you are starting to get into other people's 'stuff'!" But if I am working the program on a daily basis, they will see it, feel it, and I can share what I have learned in S-Anon with my children at their level.

Reconciliation and Healing... One of the first things I had to deal with in recovery was my overwhelming shame and guilt over how my part in this disease affected my children. At that point, they were already grown up; one of my children had not spoken to me for two years, and the other two were wary, to say the least. Their father was not a sexaholic, but my disease was fully present when I was married to him, and grew worse over the years. The best of my efforts and attention were always focused on my partner, and I neglected my children emotionally and physically.

When I felt ready to face their possible rejection, I told my children as much as they wanted to know about the past, and their reactions were as individual as they are. One daughter wanted to know all about it, my son showed very little desire to hear my story, and my younger daughter asked a question here and there, and then cut off the discussion abruptly when she had heard as much as she could handle for the moment. My current husband's involvement in his recovery program for sexaholics was mentioned in passing, but the details of his old behaviors seemed irrelevant as far as my children were concerned. It was my obsession with my partners that affected them.

As the years have passed, I have sensed our children's growing respect for my husband's and my recovery. It fills me with joy to realize that we have become the kind of parents to whom they can turn with their problems, knowing that we have faced and overcome some really tough issues, one day at a time. Today, even the problems related to my children [and grandchildren!] are a luxury that at one point in my life I believed I would never enjoy. I also know that the most valuable gift I can give them is the gift of my ongoing, One-Day-at-a-Time S-Anon recovery.

Protecting Each Other?... After years of protecting my husband, I told my teenagers about my S-Anon recovery and explained that the disease of sexaholism was present in our home. To my surprise, I learned that not only had the children known about my husband's affairs for years (and had kept quiet in order to "protect" me), but also that they were both angry at me for having been such a "doormat." We had our first honest conversation in years, and it was the first time we all talked about our feelings. I wish I had talked with them earlier.

Learning to Parent... Working the program in my relationship with my husband is a piece of cake when I compare it to working the program regarding my son. I constantly wrestle with questions of whether I am a controlling parent or a parent providing structure. When is detachment appropriate with my seven-year-old son and when am I allowing too much freedom? When am I providing too much information about the family addiction dynamics and when am I keeping secrets? What is normal behavior on my son's part and when is his behavior a reaction to being part of an addictive family? What makes answering these questions all the more difficult is the fact that I grew up in a dysfunctional family, so I don't have a clue as to what is "normal."

One day in an S-Anon meeting I shared these concerns with some members of the group. One member said she reads everything she can find about parenting and normal developmental stages for children. That was helpful to me, but I felt this kind of knowledge does not answer the basic question of "When am I providing guidance and when am I acting out my need to be in control?" Today when I am in the middle of a heated interchange with my son, I take some time out. If I am at home, I read recovery literature about control. If we are in public, I repeat the Serenity Prayer in my head. These actions calm me so that I can get in touch with my underlying feelings. I have been able to identify a feeling I call "wanting to shove a square peg into a round hole"—the "do it my way or else" feeling. Those are the times that I am not really parenting, but acting out my own fears by trying to controlling others.

I am a long way from being the kind of parent I would like to be, but I have become the kind of parent who can admit her shortcomings. Hopefully this will create an atmosphere in my home where things can be questioned and discussed. If my child feels safe engaging in conversation with me, I have come a long way toward healing in our relationship.

Forgiving Myself... My children were deeply affected by growing up in a home with active sexaholism. They have had to deal with some rough times and have developed some dysfunctional ways of relating to others. I am afraid that my youngest child will become an addict. My oldest child has worked through many issues and is doing much better. Today I know that I can't protect them from themselves, and I don't want to enable them either.

Feeling overwhelmed by guilt during early recovery, I continuously allowed them to blame me for their problems. I thought it would be harsh to confront them, but eventually, as I grew in my recovery, I began to see that I was enabling them to stay stuck in "blame" and "victimization." I learned that just as I cannot continue to see myself as a victim, they must abandon the victim role if they want to live happy and healthy lives. I cannot accept their accusations and continue to live in shame and guilt, while trying to stay "sober" in my recovery. I have had to just let go and let God.

S-Anon has taught me that I did the best I could with the tools and skills handed down to me by my parents. I believe I will always feel some pain, wishing I had gotten into recovery earlier. When I finally forgave myself, it was a great relief. I have learned to look at what is going on with my children as a part of their "journey" in life, knowing that no one escapes the problems inherent in his/her own journey. I cannot afford to enable them by accepting the blame for all their troubles. I know they are doing the best they can at this time, and I pray for them both, knowing they both have a deep and abiding faith in God. Today, I validate their feelings—but I also tell them that it is their right to feel the way they do—but also tell them that I hope that one day they will choose to stop feeling victimized; and as adults, get help and move on.

Honesty is the Key... I believe my children should be treated with dignity and respect—just as I want them to treat me and others. Keeping that principle in mind, I continue to dialogue with my children on a very regular basis about what is happening in our individual lives as well as in our family life. I hopefully utilize the principles of the program when I am doing this. Also, I began taking my children to Twelve Step meetings for teenagers prior to telling them anything about my addictions or my codependency. My programs support me as a parent in my journey of recovery. I did not, nor do I today, ask my children if they want to go to a recovery meeting for teens; I just take them there. I believe that is part of my job as a recovering parent. It is their responsibility to attend. Meetings and recovery may be optional, but they will only get to "choose" to recover when they are old enough to be on their own. For today, as part of this family, we are all expected to attend those meetings. This is a program of action.

I began to talk with my daughter, now almost 17, when she turned 11. I shared that I attend the S-Anon Program. I gave examples of what I was like prior to S-Anon. I pointed out examples of my character defects in action. I let my children know that I am willing to answer any of their questions with dignity and respect, but I will not share inappropriate details.

I have been equally honest with my children about other topics. My mother, who has both Alzheimer's and Parkinson's disease, lives with us. We routinely discuss her medical problems in a manner which gives both children understanding of her behaviors and needs. I also use this approach regarding my own medical problems and personal needs. The children understand the basics well and are able to incorporate the information into their lives. I respect my children's intellectual and emotional capabilities. I trust that their Higher Power and their program will help them understand what I am trying to share.

Carrying the Message... Talking to my children about S-Anon has been an on-going process. During my early years in the program, I told my children I needed the support of the group to help me work through the pain I felt from broken trust and infidelity in my marriage. When I did my initial Step work, I offered my children amends for my attempts to control their lives, my emotional unavailability, and the inappropriate anger I directed toward them.

My talks with my children focused on the support S-Anon gave me to change my destructive behaviors. As my children grew into adolescence, I shared more about our family's history with addictions and the disease process. Now my children are adults and have heard me speak about the S-Anon Program for half of their lives. It has been a gift to share the message of S-Anon with my children. I am grateful God has guided the timings of our talks and given me the words to carry the message.

• • •

MEMBERS SHARE—RELATIONSHIPS WITH
EXTENDED FAMILY AND FRIENDS

Dealing with Shame… When my husband first admitted he was a sexaholic and began to attend a program for his recovery, he was so excited to finally understand the nature of his problem that he told several of our friends about his affairs and his new recovery program. I was so ashamed and embarrassed! I imagined them thinking that I must not have been a very good sexual partner or else he would not have been interested in other women. I was positive they thought his affairs were my fault, no matter what he told them about having a disease. At that time I was not yet in S-Anon and did not even realize I might need recovery for myself.

S-Anon has taught me that I am not responsible for my husband's problem, and that what I think about me matters much more than what others think. When I talk with my friends or family members about my S-Anon Program, I say that I have an illness just as my husband does. My illness made me think that I was to blame for his behavior, it made me try to control him sexually and in other ways, and it made me feel like a failure because I was unable to do so. I was so afraid of being alone and had such a low opinion of myself that I didn't think I had any real choices in my life. These are issues I work on in S-Anon.

Establishing Boundaries… I used to believe that I had to answer any personal question that was asked of me. I would read newspaper advice columns and wonder how people got the courage to tell other people to "mind their own business" if they asked a question that was too personal. It seemed impossible to me. I can't say that in recovery I go around telling everyone to mind their own business, but I'm learning how to say things like "Oh, that's a long story" or "Please, don't get me started." Now I understand that I don't owe my friends or family any explanation. I may come to the point where I want to share certain things with them, but when to share with them and how much to tell are decisions that are mine to make. Another sentence that I have learned to say is, "I don't want to talk about that right now." For me, that is recovery!

Maintaining Honesty with Anonymity... In my desire to be honest with very close friends about the growth I was experiencing from attending S-Anon meetings, I just referred to them as "Twelve-Step" meetings. I said I was learning about how to let go of my tendencies toward not taking care of myself and my excessive need to control, especially in my relationship with my husband. If they asked if he was in a program, I just told them that it was his story to tell, not mine.

Gifts of Sharing... Before coming to S-Anon, I didn't really know what a boundary was. I tended to share my whole life story with people I would meet, not waiting to see if they were trustworthy or even interested. That characteristic was still with me when I came to S-Anon, so I just started sharing a "new chapter" with people. Looking back I can see now how inappropriate much of my sharing was. I often broke my husband's anonymity and told graphic and completely unnecessary details about his behavior and mine. I told friends and family members indiscriminately because I thought the information could "help" them. Telling friends and family has helped lessen my shame about being involved with a sexaholic. Now friends and family know my story and what I've done, and all but a few still accept me. Most even respect me more for working through my situation rather than running from it. For me, I feel that sharing my story—however imperfectly—truly has helped me come a long way in recovery.

In the program I've come to understand what boundaries are and why it's important to have them. I've learned to tell my story selectively, and to only tell details as appropriate. In fact, now I usually speak in general terms because that is often enough. It has definitely been "Progress, not Perfection," though, as I've made plenty of mistakes along the way. For example, shortly after getting into the program I told my sister about our situation because I was concerned about her relationship with her boyfriend. I shared much more than was necessary, and then told her what she "ought" to do. Of course she was put off! But in the end my vulnerability in sharing brought us closer than we've ever been.

My Needs Count... I spent years covering up my partner's sexual acting out and protecting him. Even though I experienced severe emotional pain over his affairs, fear of disease due to his involvement with prostitutes, anger over money spent on pornography and telephone calls, and shame over his arrests, I was afraid to get help for myself because of what people would think about my husband. But I'm learning that my needs count! I'm learning to find safe places where I can share my problems and the program. As a recovering S-Anon member, I often cannot avoid mentioning, in general terms, something about my husband's problem, but there is no need to go into detail. In S-Anon, we learn to place the focus on ourselves and our own recovery, and that's what I share with others.

CARRYING THE S-ANON
MESSAGE

⚭

We may learn about S-Anon recovery at meetings, by reading S-Anon Conference Approved Literature, and/or sharing with S-Anon members by telephone and email. When we keep coming back to S-Anon, we hear what members were like before S-Anon and how they have changed as a result of working the S-Anon Program. We find hope and courage to work S-Anon's Twelve Steps for ourselves. We become able to share our own experiences within the group, with a sponsor, or perhaps with another S-Anon member. We, too, begin to carry the S-Anon message.

We are grateful for the S-Anon members who have gone before us, for willingly sharing the message of their recovery. Carrying the message is how we give to others what has so generously been given to us. We learn that in order to keep growing and having the support we desire, we need to give it away to others. In S-Anon we receive help when we hear stories of recovery, as well as when we share our own.

Carrying the message is often referred to as Twelfth Step work. The Twelfth Step states: *Having had a spiritual awakening as the result of these Steps, we tried to carry this message to others, and to practice these principles in all our affairs.* When we begin to see the possibilities that our Higher Power and participation in this fellowship have to offer to us, we can begin to share them with others. It is often suggested that we work the Twelve Steps in order, and for the sake of our own recovery we not skip certain steps or get overly involved with others. We can; however, begin to work the Twelfth Step, even while we continue working the other Steps.

As we start to practice the principles of the S-Anon Program, positive changes occur in our perspectives and actions. At times our progress seems slow, but we learn to appreciate progress and not demand perfection. Sometimes it takes a while to understand the various principles. We find that we can revisit certain Steps or apply them to additional aspects of our lives. We learn to trust the guidance and timing of our Higher Power to help us become aware of attitudes and behaviors that stand in the way of our recovery. Our sponsor or another S-Anon member can often help us, too. We begin to experience our Higher Power's gift of serenity, and our confusion, fear, and depression lessen. In this way we carry the message of our recovery to S-Anon members, and to others, as well.

Sometimes we find it difficult to share our S-Anon recovery outside of S-Anon. Some of us find that many of our family members and friends do not understand our situation. At those times we often find it best to work the S-Anon principles quietly and let our actions carry the message. We also find that however and whenever we share, we are not in control of how other people receive our stories or experience. We leave the results in our Higher Power's hands, trusting that others also have a Higher Power leading them in their own time and way.

Carrying the message of S-Anon may include sharing at meetings, being a sponsor, or doing service at any level—personal, meeting, local, Intergroup, regional, or World Service. We only need to have honesty, open-mindedness, and willingness to share. By carrying the message to others, we can keep what we have been given.

SHARING AT MEETINGS

"There are many ways to carry the message. The changes in our lives speak the loudest. We can be ready to answer anyone who may notice and inquire as to how those changes came about. Also, we bring our message to others each time we share in a meeting or stay after the meeting to talk to newcomers. We carry our message when we make telephone calls or perform service of any kind for the group."[8]

Sharing at meetings is one type of Twelfth-Step work. We do not need many years of recovery or a gift for public speaking in order to carry the message. There is no need to worry about saying the right thing. We just speak from the heart about how we are using or trying to use the tools of the program in our own lives. We try to focus on the solution and the experience, strength, and hope we are finding in S-Anon, rather than on specific details about our problems. We seldom share all the details about our situation at our S-Anon meeting. Instead, we can share more specifics with our sponsor or another member at another time.

It takes courage to share at meetings. We may have trouble trusting others with what we have to share. We have varied experiences of being affected by sexaholism and sometimes feel isolated. The important thing is that we want to recover from the effects on us of another person's sexual addiction.

Tradition Eleven states: *Our public relations policy is based on attraction rather than promotion; we need always maintain personal anonymity at the level of press, radio, TV and films. We need guard with special care the anonymity of all S-Anon and SA members.*

Tradition Twelve states: *Anonymity is the spiritual foundation of all our Traditions, ever reminding us to place principles above personalities.* These Traditions remind us to respect anonymity. Anonymity is a very important concept for S-Anon members to understand and

---

[8] *S-Anon Twelve Steps*, p. 144

remember. More information on anonymity is on pages 43 and 44 of this book as well as in the summary of the Traditions.

By honestly describing our own path toward spiritual growth and recovery, we become living proof that the program works. We truly are all miracles. Because we know first-hand the pain of living with the disease of sexaholism, we can often bring hope to the newcomer when others cannot.

Some of us may work another recovery program as well as be affected by the sexaholism of a relative or friend. Regardless of our other affiliations, we are all welcome to attend S-Anon meetings. Tradition Three states: *....The only requirement for membership is that there be a problem of sexaholism in a relative or friend.* Our meeting guidelines suggest that our other program identities remain anonymous and that we focus our sharing on our S-Anon recovery. During S-Anon meetings we use only S-Anon Conference Approved Literature and leave our other identities outside, such as other Twelve Step issues, philosophies, religions, therapies, and occupations. These guidelines help to minimize distractions that can divert us from our primary spiritual aim of S-Anon recovery. Information about sharing our experience with newcomers can be found later in this Part of the book.

Finding My Voice... When I attended my first S-Anon meetings, I could only listen. My voice just choked up when I simply tried to read any of the opening meeting materials. I listened to others share things to which I could and sometimes could not relate. I liked that the group members said, "Thank you." after someone shared. I could say, "Thank you." I said it with heartfelt gratitude, because I was hearing some things that I could not express. I also appreciated that when some members shared, we laughed as we identified with things we had also done or felt. Eventually, I was able to share within the group. Sharing helps my own recovery, and when I share, people thank me. I am grateful that my sharing may help someone else. I understand better today that this is a way I can carry the message of my own recovery.

Safe Place... When I first began attending S-Anon meetings I was furious. I would show up in my home group every Sunday night, cross my arms and make my proclamation: "I hate this; I hate being here." For a solid year I used my voice and stated how I felt. It was the first time in my life that I actually felt anger and was able to voice that anger in a safe place. No one tried to fix me or tell me I couldn't be angry. I got a sponsor and started working the Twelve Steps right way. Eventually the anger just went away. When I share my story now, I tell about my anger and how working the Twelve Steps has brought me peace.

Honest Sharing... I often pray for courage to be honest at meetings. It can be sometimes difficult for me to admit that my behavior is not always commendable. I tend to be a perfectionist and want to put on my best face. When I hear others sharing honestly, it is so helpful to me. I want to do the same. I want to share my "news" and not my "views." (I learned that from an old time program member.) Even if my news is not as pretty as I would like, I find that when I am honest I am progressing in my recovery. I trust that my honest sharing carries the message of recovery. Hearing honest sharing helps me to understand how the program works.

SERVICE WITHIN THE GROUP

Another way we work the Twelfth Step is to do service work in our "home" group (the group we attend regularly — the one in which we feel most comfortable). We can help set up the chairs and literature before the meeting, serve as the meeting leader, contact people who inquire about our program, or volunteer to be a trusted servant such as the group secretary or treasurer. Any activity that makes it possible for the meeting to take place and to be a source of hope and recovery for a newcomer is Twelfth Step work. If we start an S-Anon meeting in our area, we will serve ourselves, and also others who may be suffering alone and may one day search for an S-Anon group. Doing service in groups that meet via electronic media (i.e. telephone and internet) is also an opportunity to carry the message of S-Anon.

Accepting a service position is an opportunity to grow in our understanding of how to apply the Twelve Traditions to our group and to our lives. S-Anon's Twelve Traditions, which are briefly highlighted in Part One of this book, are guidelines for the health of our groups. When we use the Twelve Traditions to guide us, we find it possible to conduct healthy meetings. We have found that an ongoing study of the Twelve Traditions and sharing about them in our meeting discussions can minimize situations that can destroy a group.

You can read more about service on page 20-22. The suggested format for meetings and a list of Conference Approved readings are in Part 4 of this book as well as in the *S-Anon/S-Ateen Service Manual*. Other supportive materials for starting a meeting are available from the S-Anon World Service Office.

Little Things Matter... As a newcomer, when I heard about carrying the message to others, I thought, "That will be a fine trick! How can I carry the message of S-Anon to someone else when I can't even talk about this to anybody?" I thought it would be an impossible task for me. I learned after a little time in the program that we can just take one step at a time, so I volunteered to bring coffee to the meeting. It really did make me feel more a part of the group.

Progress Not Perfection... I volunteered to be the key holder for my Saturday night meeting. The church had asked us not to duplicate the key, so I was the only one with a key. I admit that I can be forgetful. Well, one week I forgot the key. We were a small meeting , so we actually met in my car that night. Thankfully, I found the key before the next meeting. It was a comfort to know I didn't have to be perfect in order to do service. I felt appreciated and appreciate others who take turns holding the key.

SPONSORSHIP

In the very early days of AA, a newcomer had to be "sponsored" before she or he could even attend an AA meeting. Today this concept has changed a great deal, and we find that sponsorship means different things to different people. In S-Anon, sponsorship is a key kind of Twelfth Step work. Sponsors are program members who can help us work the Steps by sharing how they have worked or are working these Steps in their own lives. A sponsor is also a person with whom we feel comfortable enough to share our whole story and who is willing to guide us on our journey through the Twelve Steps. No one is required to have a sponsor. Our experience suggests; however, that in order to minimize confusion and frustration it it is most helpful to rely on one person in S-Anon who knows our situation well. Working the Steps with a sponsor also encourages us to maintain accountability while on our recovery journey.

Many members have found it difficult to ask for this kind of help, and even more difficult to listen to and apply any suggestions that may be offered. Once these initial obstacles are overcome, a sponsor can be a real source of strength and inspiration. Newcomers sometimes feel that they don't want to be a bother to another member or may feel embarrassed to ask for help in understanding the principles of the program. Many members who have sponsored others are grateful for the experience and for how it has enhanced their own growth in recovery.

There is no right or wrong way to be a sponsor. Having worked through at least the first five Steps and having our own sponsor is often good preparation to be a sponsor. The usual guidelines apply: we don't give specific advice or tell people what to do about their personal problems. One member says, "The most important thing for me to remember in sponsoring another member is that I don't have to have all the answers. Part of me wants to rescue and fix anyone who is hurting and the other part of me knows I can't do it! I just need to stick to sharing how the tools of the program have helped me to solve my own problems. Being a sponsor can be a wonderful learning experience for S-Anon members, because sponsorship gives us a chance to put our new principles into practice. We can also see and appreciate the growth of another member from a very special viewpoint.

You may find more information on sponsorship on pages 9 - 11 of this book and in the S-Anon pamphlet, "Sponsorship in S-Anon."

Gut-Level Honesty... If other people had not been willing to share their gut-level honesty, I don't know if I'd still be here. I need to open my mouth and say something, whether I am comfortable with my thoughts and feelings or not. If I'm in a bad place, there is something for me to learn, and something for other people to learn from my bad place. It was in my sponsor/sponsee relationships where I was first able to share at this level of honesty.

Easy Does It... I know that I have a terrific need to fix people. It's like a compulsion to not mind my own business. The way I describe it is that if I don't say something to you, I'm gonna die and you're gonna die. It's gotten me into a lot of trouble, so I have to be careful that I don't push my opinions and solutions on others in the name of sharing my experience, strength, and hope. I can practice my listening skills while serving as a sponsor. Another gift I've received from working the program and being a sponsor is to learn to just look for the doors to open naturally... for God to open the door.

SERVICE BEYOND THE GROUP LEVEL

There are many opportunities for service beyond our home group. As S-Anon grows, more opportunities to be of service become available. S-Anon's Twelve Concepts of Service (adapted from Al-Anon Family Groups, Inc.), and printed in the Introductory Pages of this book, serve as guidelines for how business is conducted in S-Anon. The Concepts are also presented in the *S-Anon/ S-Ateen Service Manual*, along with the Conference Charter. S-Anon's Twelve Traditions also support us when we make decisions through a group conscience. Many of us have grown in our own recovery as we learned about these tools and principles through service. The following are some examples of areas where we may be of service:

• Contact person. With our permission, the World Service Office will give out our telephone number to new S-Anon members looking for a meeting in our area.

• Group Representative. We will participate with several other groups in our area in a Local Information Services Group— "Intergroup." An Intergroup may serve by holding local recovery events, such as S-Anon Retreats or Marathons (one-day conventions), sponsoring a contact telephone line, or reaching out to inform local helping professionals about S-Anon through mailings.

• Area Delegates to the World Service Conference help communicate an area's concerns to the annual World Service Conference where S-Anon International Family Groups, Inc. handles business that affects S-Anon as a whole.

• S-Anon Board of Trustees Standing Committees including Literature, Public Information and Outreach, Archives, International Conventions, S-Ateen, World Service Conference, and Finance. These are exciting areas of service. Often these committees meet via conference call and carry out vital services for S-Anon.

• Submitting our written experience, strength, and hope for the *S-Anews©* newsletter and other S-Anon literature is an important and valuable service to our fellowship.

• Members who have been working the S-Anon program for at least five years may serve on the S-Anon Board of Trustees. Openings on the S-Anon Board of Trustees are announced in mailings to groups, in the *S-Anews©* newsletter, and at the annual World Service Conference meeting.

Some who have served beyond the group level were reluctant, at first, to get involved as they thought they must meet some special requirement, but this is not the case. While some positions do have certain qualifications, a willingness to serve the S-Anon Fellowship is the only qualification for most volunteer positions. When considering service in S-Anon it is helpful to become familiar with the *S-Anon/S-Ateen Service Manual*. It can be wonderfully rewarding to contribute to the growth of our fellowship. You can contact the S-Anon World Service Office to find out about current service opportunities.

Gifts of Service Work... I had the strange sensation of watching myself from a distance as I raised my hand at the annual World Service Conference to volunteer to serve on the S-Anon Board of Trustees. I felt willing to serve, and I knew I had the time available, but almost immediately I began to doubt that I really had anything of value to offer, and to fear that somehow my S-Anon program and I would not be good enough. This was not a new feeling—often these same doubts and fears had kept me from getting involved in activities; but, I have discovered that the safest, most supportive way for me to confront these fears, and move past them, is to participate in S-Anon service work. The worst that can happen is that I could make a mistake, but I trust that everyone loves and will still love me anyway! The best that can happen is that my gifts and talents will be used in support of the S-Anon fellowship that saved my life. And in between, I will experience the struggle and the victory that come from learning to listen to others and respect their points of view.

Speaking up for what I believe is the right thing to do, even when I feel all alone and out on a limb. Through doing service, I have gained a deeper level of acceptance and trust that a Higher Power is looking after this fellowship. We are but "trusted servants" in every sense of those words.

New Slogans to Live By... Early in my S-Anon recovery I was comfortable and enjoyed doing service work for my home group. But I learned the most about myself and took my recovery to new levels when I did service work beyond my group. I came to recognize and develop talents I didn't even know I had. This brought up some of my faulty thinking. I had grown up hearing old slogans/tapes: *You can do that, if you just try harder; I know you will not let the family down; Do you think you are better than the others? Is your time more valuable? No excuses; You are being lazy; Can't you do what is expected of you?* and so on. In my S-Anon recovery I have heard and learned new slogans that promote gentleness and self-care. Through S-Anon service work, I have learned that it is absolutely my job, and my job alone, to look after and care for myself by setting and maintaining healthy boundaries. I've learned to respectfully say what I mean and mean what I say. I have the courage to say NO when necessary. I am very grateful for the opportunity to do this service work; I learn more about myself in the process, and give myself the gift of a more balanced life. Today I am grateful for a whole set of new slogans (such as: *Easy Does It; Keep It Simple; One Day at a Time; H.A.L.T.; Live and Let Live*) and the S-Anon program. My Higher Power continues to provide me with opportunities for me to learn and grow in my service work beyond my local group.

CONTACTING INQUIRERS

When we volunteer to serve as a contact for people who inquire about S-Anon on our local telephone contact lines or through other referral sources, it is entirely up to us how much personal anonymity we wish to maintain. We are free to tell people as much as we wish about ourselves (including our full names, addresses, or telephone numbers) but we never reveal the identity of other S-Anon members, sexaholics, or other family members without their permission.

When we first talk to inquirers, they will probably tell us something about their situation. Some may want to share a good deal about their situation, since we may be the first person with whom they have ever been able to share their story. We may also want to share something about ourselves and about how we came to the S-Anon program. One member says, "I usually ask if they are familiar with Twelve-Step programs. That provides a good starting point for the conversation and lets me know how much to say about the program itself. I can share part of my S-Anon story, so they can see if they identify with any of it." We share enough to assure them that we have had similar feelings, and that we understand how it feels to be reaching out for help because we've been there, too.

If they express interest in coming to meetings, we give them information about times and locations and encourage them to attend. We may ask if they would like to meet briefly before the meeting starts or have us accompany them to their first meeting. This can help a newcomer feel more comfortable. Giving newcomers an opportunity to ask questions or share about their situation with one or several S-Anon members is often helpful. When we refer anyone to a particular S-Anon group that we do not regularly attend, it may be helpful to let a member of that group know that a newcomer may be there. We may remember how much courage it took for us to walk into our first S-Anon meeting.

SHARING EXPERIENCE, STRENGTH, AND HOPE WITH NEWCOMERS

We find that careful listening with our hearts and our heads can help us to share with newcomers in a loving way. As we discover the things they are most concerned about, we can focus our sharing on those areas. The following are some typical areas of sharing:

1. We can share how we found hope for our own recovery in S-Anon. We can tell them about our First Step experience of powerlessness and surrender.

2. We can let them know that they are not alone—at one time or another we have all felt the anger, guilt, shame, or hopelessness that they may be feeling now.

3. We can share that S-Anon has shown us that we do have choices, so we need not feel trapped in an impossible situation. Sharing with and listening to other group members shows us that no sit-

uation is really hopeless and helps us to put our own problems in perspective.

4. We can emphasize that this is an anonymous program, and explain what "anonymity" means in S-Anon. We go to great lengths to protect one another's anonymity—and that of sexaholics and family members as well. We also assure newcomers that any personal information they share will be kept in confidence.

5. If they do not have a meeting in their area, we can offer some general suggestions as to how to break out of the isolation that most of us have felt, and how to find people to support them. The World Service Office (WSO) may be able to provide them with a telephone sponsor and information on meetings that may be available through electronic media. The WSO also can provide information and support for them to eventually start a meeting.

6. If the person is completely new to Twelve-Step programs, we might talk about the following ideas: a) We believe sexaholism is a disease very similar to alcoholism. This means that the actions of the sexaholic are not a result of something we have or have not done. b) S-Anon recovery is based upon spiritual principles. We rely upon a Power greater than ourselves to restore us to sanity. c) No one individual speaks for the entire S-Anon Fellowship. d) We suggest that they try to attend at least 6 meetings before they decide if S-Anon is for them.

7. We can encourage them to read S-Anon Conference Approved Literature. We may describe what books are available and where to get them. It may be helpful to have S-Anon Conference Approved Literature, such as the newcomer booklet, "We're Glad You're Here," available for reference when sharing with inquirers and newcomers. We can read portions to them if it seems appropriate.

8. Some newcomers ask about how much to tell extended family members and friends. This can be a sensitive issue. Our experience suggests that keeping secrets may be unhealthy, but also we have learned that there is wisdom in not giving too much information to those who do not need to know it. We try to remember to take our time and not share too much too soon. S-Anon experience suggests that it is best not to tell others if we are doing it solely to ease our pain or vent our anger. Newcomers may want to inform health professionals and undergo tests for sexually transmitted diseases.

It is important that we speak only as S-Anon members, sharing the experience, strength, and hope we have gained through our own recovery in S-Anon. We do not give advice or analyze the personal situations of others. We do not speak as counselors, therapists, or experts in the field of addiction, even if that is our profession outside the fellowship. We simply speak as people who have found hope and recovery by working the S-Anon Program.

We gain so much for our own recovery when we share our experience, strength, and hope with others. In fact, most of us agree that we have received much more help than we have given. In sharing, we often realize how grateful we are for the program and for the changes it has made in our lives. We see our own recovery more clearly as we recognize ourselves in the newcomer, and remember how our lives used to be. Many of us have felt more humble, too. Our task is merely to carry the message; we realize that the outcome of our efforts lies in the hands of a Power greater than ourselves.

Actions Share a Message... In my S-Anon recovery, I knew that all I needed to do was to share my own experience, strength, and hope. I recognized that the timing and individual progress were up to the newcomers and their Higher Power. I was glad to know it was not my responsibility. When my daughter disclosed her sexaholism to me, she said she felt comfortable and able to do so because she felt safe. She saw for herself what working the Twelve Steps, consulting with a sponsor, attending meetings regularly, etc. had done for me. She had "witnessed" my transformation not only in dealing with her father's disease of sexaholism, but also in my willingness to work on my family of origin issues. I had carried the message of my recovery without knowing it! My actions had spoken louder than any words I could have used. I am grateful.

Walking in the Light... Every time I share about my experiences with sexaholism and what happened to me throughout my childhood, my adult life, and my marriage the pain decreases. I can see more clearly now that I am speaking the truth about my situation. I had been in denial about those experiences prior to my S-Anon recovery. I knew I had been living a lie, but I didn't want to admit it. When I allowed the light and the truth to come in, I found a brand new life waiting for me.

Carrying the message has helped me to heal. When I speak the truth, the truth sets me free. That is a spiritual principle that always works for me. Carrying the message of my truth to others is like turning on the light in a dark room. The darkness just goes. I love to carry this message of hope and recovery.

S-ANON MEETING
MATERIALS

CﬓЬ

S-ANON MEETING FORMAT

"Although it may seem repetitive or time-consuming to hear the
same readings in the same order at every meeting before the individual sharing begins, it can be helpful for a number of reasons.
One reason is that it gives information to newcomers. Another reason is that no matter how many times we may have heard a particular piece read aloud, the next time we hear it may be the
moment our growth in the program allows us to understand it in
a new and helpful way. The readings also create a "buffer zone"
between the outside world and the meeting, allowing us to turn
our thoughts away from everyday concerns toward our spiritual
growth and recovery." [8]

SUGGESTED FORMAT FOR AN S-ANON MEETING

E xplanatory note: Meetings should open and close on time, but
there is no rigid formula for an S-Anon meeting. This Suggested
Meeting Format is included because most new groups find a general outline to be helpful, especially if no one in the group has
attended any Twelve-Step meetings. The format is printed for your

---

[8]*S-Anon/S-Ateen Service Manual, 2007,* p. 18

convenience. Because S-Anon groups are autonomous, not every group chooses to plan its meeting in this way. However, this format is Conference Approved, which means that it reflects the experience of a wide variety of S-Anon individuals and groups.

We suggest that you try it, and then adapt or vary the format to suit the needs of your group. We ask only that you keep in mind that "adaptation" does not mean substituting readings from material that has not been Conference Approved (Tradition One), or changing any words in the S-Anon Conference Approved suggested readings, S-Anon Twelve Steps, or S-Anon Twelve Traditions. (At the date of printing for this book, literature published by S-Anon, SA, Al-Anon, and AA is Conference Approved for use in our meetings.) Helpful suggestions for successful meetings can be found in Part 1 and Appendix D of the *S-Anon/S-Ateen Service Manual* and the companion pages "How to Start a Meeting." The suggested format of an S-Anon meeting appears below, and the suggested readings follow. (The suggested formats for S-Anon and S-Ateen meetings can be found in the *S-Anon/S-Ateen Service Manual* and are available on the website.)

1. **Will those who care to join me in a moment of silence, followed by the Serenity Prayer?**

   [Serenity Prayer is said.]

2. **Hi, I'm_____, your leader for this meeting.**

   [To open the meeting, The S-Anon Welcome may be read.]

3. **The Preamble to the Twelve Steps of S-Anon describes the purpose of our Group:**
   [Preamble to the Twelve Steps of S-Anon may be read by the Leader or another member.]

4. **Here are the Twelve Steps we follow which are suggested for our recovery:**

[The Twelve Steps of S-Anon are read. Many groups pass a copy of the Steps around the group and each member reads one (or more) of them.]

5. **Our group experience suggests that the unity of the S-Anon Family Groups depends upon our adherence to the following Traditions:**

[The Twelve Traditions are read; some groups read only the Tradition that corresponds to the month, for example, January —First Tradition.]

6. **Newcomer Welcome**

[At this point in the meeting, many groups have the Leader ask if there are newcomers present and if so, extend a further welcome as decided by the group members, assuring them that they are free to share or remain silent, as they wish. If a Newcomer Meeting is available, that information can be given at this point. Some groups set aside a specific time at the end of the meeting for newcomers' questions and concerns.]

7. **Introduction by First Name**

[Group members introduce themselves by first name. Some groups wait until later in the meeting, after the announcements, to introduce themselves and join in saying the Serenity Prayer, so that those who come in after the meeting has started can be included.]

8. **We are seeking recovery from our own progressive illness:**

[The short or long version of the S-Anon Problem may be read at this time.]

9. **Our recovery depends upon our willingness to adopt new ways of thinking about ourselves and our problems:**

[The short or long version of the Keys to S-Anon Recovery may be read at this time.]

10. **There are three Obstacles to Recovery in S-Anon:**

[Obstacles to Recovery may be read at this time.]

11. **Our Seventh Tradition states that "Every group ought to be fully self-supporting, declining outside contributions." We have no dues or fees for membership. The Seventh Tradition collection is used to cover group expenses and to support S-Anon local and world services.**

[Pass basket. For the benefit of newcomers, many groups say something like, "If this is your first meeting, we would like you to be our guest and not contribute." Some groups pass two baskets, one for group expenses, and one to support S-Anon Twelfth-Step work at the national and international level. Some groups wait until the end of the meeting to ask for Seventh Tradition contributions.]

12. **Announcements and Secretary/Treasurer reports.**

[Leader asks if there are any S-Anon-related announcements or a Secretary or Treasurer's report. Announcements could also be made at the end of the meeting or during the passing of the Seventh Tradition Basket.]

13. **Meeting Guidelines**

[Before sharing begins, Leader reads the following:]

Because our common welfare comes first, here are the guidelines for sharing during our meeting:

If you wish to share, please wait your turn to share or wait to be recognized by the leader, as there is no crosstalk. That is, we share with the group as a whole, rather than addressing comments or questions to individual members. We limit the length of our sharing so that everyone here will have a chance to speak. Our purpose in sharing is to discuss ourselves, not the sexaholic. Our meetings focus on the S-Anon approach to recovery, so we avoid the mention or discussion of specific titles and authors of publications other than S-Anon Conference Approved Literature. We leave our other identities outside the discussion — other Twelve-Step issues, philosophies, religions, therapies and occupations. We speak about and from the S-Anon point of view. Each member of the group is encouraged to remind other members, during the meeting if necessary, of our commitment to these guidelines.

[These are the guidelines that S-Anon International Family Groups have found to serve the recovery of all the members. They provide information to newcomers and serve as a reminder to all group members so that our meetings stay focused on recovery and provide a safe place to share feelings without having to explain or justify them. While all groups may not use these exact words, it is important that the guidelines you do use are supported by a group conscience of the members, and that a substantial majority of group members are committed to upholding them.]

14. Leader Qualifies (Optional):

[Sometimes the meeting leader spends five minutes or less "qualifying" (talking about his/her membership in S-Anon), with a limit of five minutes or less. They tell, from a recovery point of view, what they were like before S-Anon, how they have changed, and generally share experience, strength, and hope in coming to terms with the family disease of sexaholism.]

15. Meeting Opened for Sharing

[Leader announces the format of the meeting (for example, a Step or Tradition Meeting) or introduces the topic.]

16. Closing Reminder

[When it is time for the meeting to end, the Leader reads the following:]

This is an anonymous program. We ask all members to respect our anonymity. The stories you hear are told in confidence and should not be repeated outside the meeting, including to spouses or family members. They are told so that we might better understand this program and ourselves, and to give encouragement and help to the newcomer, so that we may keep what we have been given.

17. The Gifts of the S-Anon Program

[The Gifts of the S-Anon Program may be read at this time.]

18. Will those who care to, join us in the closing prayer:

[Leader asks someone to lead the group in saying the Serenity Prayer, Third Step Prayer, or other prayer from S-Anon Conference Approved Literature, as determined by the group.]

KEEP COMING BACK! IT WORKS IF YOU WORK IT!

SUGGESTED READINGS FOR
S-ANON MEETINGS

THE SERENITY PRAYER

God grant me the serenity
To accept the things I cannot change,
Courage to change the things I can,
And wisdom to know the difference.

THE S-ANON WELCOME

We welcome you to the_____S-Anon Family Group and hope that in this fellowship you will find the help and friendship that we have been privileged to enjoy. We would like you to feel that we understand as perhaps few can. We too were lonely and frustrated; but here we have found that there is no situation too difficult to be bettered, and no unhappiness too great to be lessened.

The S-Anon Family Groups consist of relatives and friends of sexaholics who realize that by banding together they can better solve their common problems. We urge you to try our program. Without spiritual help, living with, or having lived with, a sexaholic is too much for most of us. We become nervous, irritable, and unreasonable; our thinking becomes confused, and our perspective becomes distorted. Rarely have we seen a person who was not greatly benefitted by working the S-Anon program. The Twelve Steps of S-Anon which we try to follow are not easy. At first we may think that some of them are unnecessary, but if we are honest, open-minded, and willing to apply the principles of the Twelve Steps to our lives, we find that the benefits can be limitless, including God's gift of serenity.

S-ANON PREAMBLE TO THE TWELVE STEPS

S-Anon is a fellowship of people who share their experience, strength, and hope with each other so that they may solve their common problems and help others to recover. The only requirement for membership is that there be a problem of sexaholism in a relative or friend. There are no dues or fees for S-Anon membership; we are   self-supporting   through   our   own   contributions. S-Anon is not allied with any sect, denomination, politics, organization, or institution; does not wish to engage in any controversy; neither endorses nor opposes any causes. Our primary purpose is to recover from the effects upon us of another person's sexaholism and to help families and friends of sexaholics.

THE TWELVE STEPS OF S-ANON

1. We admitted we were powerless over sexaholism—that our lives had become unmanageable.

2. Came to believe that a Power greater than ourselves could restore us to sanity.

3. Made a decision to turn our will and our lives over to the care of God *as we understood Him.*

4. Made a searching and fearless moral inventory of ourselves.

5. Admitted to God, to ourselves, and to another human being the exact nature of our wrongs.

6. Were entirely ready to have God remove all these defects of character.

7. Humbly asked Him to remove our shortcomings.

8. Made a list of all persons we had harmed, and became willing to make amends to them all.

9. Made direct amends to such people wherever possible, except when to do so would injure them or others.

10. Continued to take personal inventory and when we were wrong promptly admitted it.

11. Sought through prayer and meditation to improve our conscious contact with God *as we understood Him,* praying only for knowledge of His will for us and the power to carry that out.

12. Having had a spiritual awakening as the result of these Steps, we tried to carry this message to others, and to practice these principles in all our affairs.

THE TWELVE STEPS OF
ALCOHOLICS ANONYMOUS:

1. We admitted we were powerless over alcohol — that our lives had become unmanageable. 2. Came to believe that a Power greater than ourselves could restore us to sanity. 3. Made a decision to turn our will and our lives over to the care of God *as we understood Him.* 4. Made a searching and fearless moral inventory of ourselves. 5. Admitted to God, to ourselves, and to another human being the exact nature of our wrongs. 6. Were entirely ready to have God remove all these defects of character. 7. Humbly asked Him to remove our shortcomings. 8. Made a list of all persons we had harmed, and became willing to make amends to them all. 9. Made direct amends to such people wherever possible, except when to do so would injure them or others. 10. Continued to take personal inventory and when we were wrong promptly admitted it. 11. Sought through prayer and meditation to improve our conscious contact with God *as we understood Him,* praying only for knowledge of His will for us and the power to carry that out. 12. Having had a spiritual awakening as the result of these Steps, we tried to carry this message to alcoholics, and to practice these principles in all our affairs.

(The Twelve Steps and Twelve Traditions reprinted and adapted with permission of Alcoholics Anonymous World Services, Inc. Permission to reprint and adapt the Steps and Traditions does not mean that AA is affiliated with this program. AA is a program of recovery from alcoholism — use of this material in connection with programs which are patterned after AA, but which address other problems, does not imply otherwise.)

TWELVE TRADITIONS OF S-ANON

Our group experience suggests that the unity of the S-Anon Family Groups depends upon our adherence to the following Traditions:

1. Our common welfare should come first; personal progress for the greatest number depends upon unity.

2. For our group purpose there is but one authority—a loving God as He may express Himself in our group conscience. Our leaders are but trusted servants—they do not govern.

3. The relatives of sexaholics, when gathered together for mutual aid, may call themselves an S-Anon Family Group, provided that, as a group, they have no other affiliation. The only requirement for membership is that there be a problem of sexaholism in a relative or friend.

4. Each group should be autonomous, except in matters affecting another group or S-Anon or SA as a whole.

5. Each S-Anon Family Group has but one purpose: to help families of sexaholics. We do this by practicing the Twelve Steps of S-Anon, by encouraging and understanding our sexaholic relatives, and by welcoming and giving comfort to the families of sexaholics.

6. Our S-Anon Family Groups ought never endorse, finance, or lend our name to any outside enterprise, lest problems of money, property, and prestige divert us from our primary spiritual aim. Although a separate entity, we should always cooperate with Sexaholics Anonymous.

7. Every group ought to be fully self-supporting, declining outside contributions.

8. S-Anon Twelfth Step work should remain forever non-professional, but our service centers may employ special workers.

9. Our groups, as such, ought never be organized; but we may create service boards or committees directly responsible to those they serve.

10. The S-Anon Family Groups have no opinion on outside issues; hence our name ought never be drawn into public controversy.

11. Our public relations policy is based on attraction rather than promotion; we need always maintain personal anonymity at the level of press, radio, TV, and films. We need guard with special care the anonymity of all S-Anon and SA members.

12. Anonymity is the spiritual foundation of all our Traditions, ever reminding us to place principles above personalities.

THE S-ANON PROBLEM
(Short Version)

S-Anon members have much in common with the friends and relatives of other addicted people. Most of us grew up in families with secrets, and we were not taught to think about our own needs and take positive action to meet them. We chose friends and partners who could not or would not love and support us in a healthy way. We lived life from the standpoint of victims and perceived any personal criticism as a threat. For most of us, anger, fear, and depression were nearly constant. We acquired some unhealthy beliefs about ourselves very early in our lives—that we were not worthwhile and lovable, that we were able to control other people's behavior, and that sex was the most important sign of love.

We have also felt the shame of thinking we were responsible for the sexaholic behavior of a family member or friend. Our self-esteem dropped to low levels, and we doubted our attractiveness, our emotions, and our sanity. We have felt betrayed by those we loved the most. Many of us were sexually abused, exposed to diseases, and otherwise placed in physical danger. We were often too ashamed to ask for help.

Some of us minimized the importance of the sexaholic behavior or denied it until we felt emotionally numb. Others focused on the sexaholic behavior to the point of obsession and tried every known method to control it. Some of us participated in sexual behavior that made us ashamed of ourselves or used sex to manipulate the sexaholic. Some of us misused drugs, alcohol, or food, and others kept so busy that we didn't have time to feel our emotions. We often neglected our health, our jobs, and our children. No matter how we tried to struggle against it, deny it, or minimize its effects, the failure of our efforts to cope with sexaholism brought us to the point of despair. This is what we mean when we say in the First Step, "our lives had become unmanageable."

THE S-ANON PROBLEM
(Long Version)

S-Anon members have much in common with the friends and
family members of other addicted people. Most of us grew up in
families with secrets, and we were not taught to think about our
own needs and take positive action to meet them. As we grew up
we felt more and more lonely and isolated as we chose friends and
partners who could not or would not love and support us in a
healthy way. We lived life from the standpoint of victims and perceived any personal criticism as a threat. For most of us, anger and
depression were a way of life. We were so afraid of being left alone
that anxiety and frustration were nearly constant. Whether or not
we were exposed to sexaholism as children, most of us think that we
acquired some unhealthy beliefs about ourselves very early in our
lives—that we were not worthwhile and loveable, that we were
able to control other people's behavior, and that sex was the most
important sign of love.

What is different is that we have felt the additional shame of
being involved with the sexaholism of a family member or friend. It
does not matter a great deal whether that person was a member of
our birth family, a partner, spouse, child, or someone outside the
family like a friend, teacher, or boss. It does not matter whether we
were willing, unwilling, or unknowing participants in the relationship—sexaholism deeply affected our lives. Our self-esteem
dropped to lower and lower levels, and we doubted our attractiveness, our emotions, our sanity, and our human worth. We have felt
betrayed by those we loved the most, and those of us who didn't
know about the sexaholic behavior felt even more humiliated and
stupid for not knowing. Many of us were sexually abused, exposed
to sexually transmitted diseases, and otherwise placed in physical
danger. We were often afraid to trust others and reach out for help
because we were afraid of what they would think of us or of the sexaholic.

Some of us reacted to sexaholism by denying its existence or
minimizing its importance. We stuffed our feelings of anger and
abandonment to the point that we felt emotionally numb. We told
ourselves things like "Everybody does this," "This shouldn't bother

me," or even "It can't be true—he or she would never do that." Others focused on the sexaholic and the sexual behavior to the point of obsession. We tried every known method to control it. We lied and covered up, spied at doorways, listened to private conversations, checked up on the sexaholic's whereabouts, read through journals and personal papers, begged, pleaded, and threatened. Some of us participated in sexual behavior that we did not enjoy or that made us ashamed of ourselves. Many of us tried to use sex to manipulate the sexaholic, thinking that being part of the acting out would give us a little bit more control over our lives. Most of us felt that we must have done something to deserve this kind of treatment, and that happiness was for others, not for us. Some of us misused drugs, alcohol, or food to numb the pain; others used activities, such as shopping, exercising, or working to keep from feeling our emotions. We often neglected our health, our jobs, and our children. No matter how we tried to struggle against it, deny it, or minimize its effects, the failure of our efforts to cope with sexaholism brought us to the point of despair. This is what we mean when we say in the First Step that "our lives had become unmanageable."

KEYS TO S-ANON RECOVERY
(Short Version)

Over time, S-Anon members learn to accept a number of new ideas: 1) Sexaholism is a disease very similar to alcoholism. At first many of us could not accept this idea. For S-Anon members, it means that we see sexaholics as sick people, not bad peo-ple. They are powerless over lust. 2) The actions of the sexaholic are not a result of something we did or did not do, and we do not have the power to control their behavior. 3) Our *attempts* to control or ignore sexual addiction led to a decline in our emotional health and may have enabled the sexaholic to continue to practice his or her disease. 4) When we first come to S-Anon, we, too, are spiritually and emotionally ill.

As we work toward full acceptance of these ideas, we begin to see our problems in a new light, and the awareness dawns that we do have choices concerning our own actions. This is the beginning of our recovery.

We remind ourselves that we are powerless over the behavior caused by sexaholism. We ask a Higher Power to help us to stop blaming and trying to control the sexaholic; the sobriety of the sexaholic is not our responsibility. We realize we cannot find serenity for ourselves if we continue to focus on someone else's recovery, so we commit ourselves to our own recovery. With the loving help of other S-Anon members and the God of our understanding, we take positive action to make our lives more serene and fulfilling. We attend as many meetings as we can, get a sponsor, if possible, and begin to apply the principles of the Twelve Steps to our lives. We use the telephone, the S-Anon literature, and the S-Anon slogans. Eventually we reach out to help others and try to carry the message of our own recovery. We do these things in our own way, one day at a time—striving for progress, not perfection. This is what is meant by "working the program."

KEYS TO S-ANON RECOVERY
(Long Version)

We accept sexaholism as a disease very similar to alcoholism. This means that we see sexaholics as sick people, not bad people. They are powerless over lust. At first many of us could not accept this idea. We thought it meant that sexaholics were somehow not responsible for their behavior, or that we were not entitled to our feelings of anger and hurt. But it does not mean either of those things. For S-Anons, it means that the actions of the sexaholic are not a result of something we did or did not do. We did not cause the sexaholic behavior by being stupid, weak, or unattractive, and we do not have the power to control it. However, as we tried to control or ignore the sexaholism in our lives, we often unknowingly acted in ways that led to a further decline in our emotional health and enabled the sexaholic to continue to practice his or her disease. Over a period of time, many of us took on the shame, guilt, and fear that characterize the disease of sexaholism, even though we may not have acted out sexually. We, too, became spiritually and emotionally ill. Once we begin to see our problems in this light, we can also see that we do have choices concerning our own behavior. This is the beginning of our recovery. As we work toward full acceptance of these ideas, we begin to see our problems in a new light, and the awareness dawns that we do have choices concerning our own actions. This is the beginning of our recovery.

We remind ourselves that we are powerless over the behavior caused by sexaholism. We ask a Higher Power to help us to stop blaming and trying to control the sexaholic; the sobriety of the sexaholic is not our responsibility. We realize we cannot find serenity for ourselves if we continue to focus on someone else's recovery, so we commit ourselves to our own recovery. With the loving help of other S-Anon members and the God of our understanding, we take positive action to make our lives more serene and fulfilling. We attend as many meetings as we can, get a sponsor, if possible, and begin to apply the principles of the Twelve Steps to our lives. We use the telephone, the S-Anon literature, and the S-Anon slogans. Eventually we reach out to help others and try to carry the message of our own recovery. We do these things in our own way, one day at a time—striving for progress, not perfection. This is what is meant by "working the program."

OBSTACLES TO RECOVERY

To insure the success of our meetings in solving our common problems, we must recognize and overcome three obstacles to recovery that can destroy the group. The first is the discussion of any religious denomination. Compulsive lusting respects no particular religion; therefore, our program is designed to help us regardless of our various beliefs. Let us not defeat our purpose by discussing any particular denomination.

The second is gossip. We are here to help ourselves and other group members. A belittling discussion of others, including the sexaholic, or a discussion of personal affairs other than those concerning ourselves, will eventually eliminate the group.

The third is dictatorship. We have no dominating authorities or self-appointed leaders. Our leaders are but trusted servants; they do not govern. We do not give advice; we suggest by telling how we solved similar problems through our experiences. The very essence of S-Anon is that the whole program is "suggested."

We have no creed, charges, obligations, or anything that would tend to hinder you. Your progress can be made in your own time and in your own way. We merely invite your attendance in a common cause.

GIFTS OF THE S-ANON PROGRAM

When we approach the process of recovery with honesty, open-mindedness, and willingness to apply the principles of the Twelve Steps to our lives, we will soon begin to see the rewards. We will become able to surrender our self-defeating behavior. We will find that we have the strength and insight to make good choices for ourselves. Our ability to act positively on behalf of our health, families, jobs, and bank accounts will amaze us. We will find that others are doing things for themselves, which we thought we had to do *for* them. Our ability to give and receive love will expand tremendously, and we will become increasingly available for loving relationships with others. We will recover the feeling of joy. We will become more honest with ourselves and experience a new comfort in our intimate relationships. We will feel the security that arises from true fellowship with others in the program, knowing that we are loved and accepted just as we are. Feelings of failure and inadequacy will be replaced by self-confidence and independence of spirit. We will no longer expect other people to provide us with an identity or a sense of self-worth. We will find the courage to be true to ourselves. We will know peace of mind and feel a stronger connection with the Higher Power of our understanding, and our Hope will turn to faith that God is really working in our lives, as we explore the wonders of serenity, dignity, and emotional growth.

INDEX